Finding Eden

A Prehistorical Novel

J. P. Kerwin

Publisher Page
an imprint of Headline Books
Terra Alta, WV

Finding Eden

by J. P. Kerwin

To order additional copies of this book or for book publishing information, or to contact the author:

Headline Books, Inc.
P.O. Box 52
Terra Alta, WV 26764
www.HeadlineBooks.com
mybook@headlinebooks.com

Publisher Page is an imprint of Headline Books

ISBN 13: 9781958914410

Library of Congress Control Number: 2024938147

PRINTED IN THE UNITED STATES OF AMERICA

To Lee
and our family

To Bill and Cathy White
from Uncle Pete
aka Joe Kerwin

Preface

This story is fiction. It's prehistoric fiction. I have imagined the world and the minds of the men and women who lived a thousand years after God awakened Adam and Eve—about ten thousand years ago. (I make no effort to unravel evolution—it's compatible with my story.) My thesis is that God—"The Maker"—gave intelligence and language to these first humans and gave them the Earth to replenish and subdue.

They were a Stone Age society. They had no writing, no metal, no medicine, no means of transportation except their feet, no domesticated animals. Lawyers, doctors, and priests were just beginning to exist. Their only means of capturing the past was to remember it.

What they believed and what happened to them is based on the great early story about it, the Book of Genesis. I take the story of Adam and Eve to be true but incomplete, and I try to comprehend it. How sin came into our lives, and by whom—Satan is a major character in the story. What he did to mankind, and how God promised not to abandon us. I think about the difference between space/time, the universe we know, and infinity/eternity, where God exists and which Satan, as Lucifer, shared before his rebellion. I suspect that the latter is much richer and more complex than we know.

These humans did the best they could. They began to learn how to feed and clothe themselves. They formed families and villages. They dealt with hardship, crime, and death but also showed courage, generosity, and love. Most importantly, they kept their faith in the Maker. It gave them hope, and it gives me hope.

1

Lucifer said, "Belial. I hear that you have news. Tell us."

Belial cooed, "I do have news. The Maker is meeting now with the human father and mother and is teaching them. Shall we join their conversation? Haste is needed."

Lucifer smiled. "That is a right good plan. To carry it out, I choose myself, in my name here, Satan, Ruler of Space and Time. With me, I require you, Belial, for knowledge and Mammon for lies. Beelzebub in reserve. Let's be on our way."

Four spirits sped away toward the small planet on the outer arm of the galaxy.

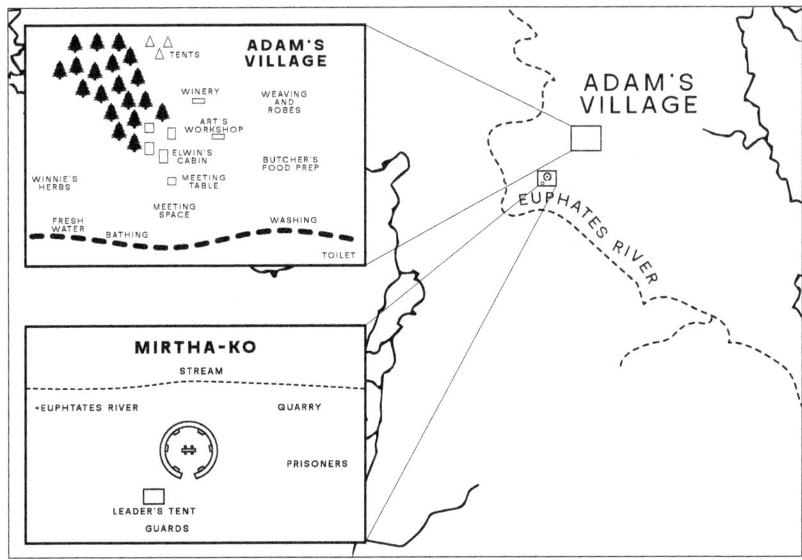

2

A thousand years went by.

Winnie emerged from her tent and swung happily down the dirt path northward toward the Council Table. She was softly singing an old tune as she went.

Squint at the sunlight, open your eye,
Sun warm wind make the little bird fly;
Sun in my eye, bird in the sky,
Wood on the fire oh baby don't cry.
Warm night firelight open your eye…

The village called Adam, whose chief was Elwin, was on high ground west of a stream that ran from the south and emptied into a tributary of the Great River, a long day's journey to the east. Trees came down the slope and gave way to a meadow near the stream. Here, at its upstream end, a few villagers were filling leather bags with fresh water.

The sun is strong today, too bright to look at, thought Winnie, smiling as she looked around at the grasses and the trees. "It's warming everything. Everything will grow!"

Tall and yellow-haired, clad in a simple robe of an animal's skin, she strode down past her own herb garden, spreading out eastward into the meadow. This was her province. Winnie was the village's expert collector of herbs. She knew all the helpful growing things—for relief of pain, healing of wounds and soothing of skin, promoting sleep or alertness, or comfort for distress. Often, she was approached by Teller, the tribe's historian and its chief healer, for medicine for a sick person; often, they came directly to her for minor afflictions.

On her left, under the trees, families had their tents, animal skins supported by tree branches; a few preferred to sleep in the open, covered by their warm leather cloaks. She passed Artisan, helping to thatch a roof. "Good morning, Art!" He turned, gave a great smile, called out, "Beautiful morning, Winnie!" She tossed her hair, gave him a glance with her pale blue eyes, and strode confidently on.

In five more minutes, she was level with the meeting place, an open field anchored on the left by the Council Table. Westward beyond the table, she could see Elwin's wooden house on the edge of the forest. Villagers would gather in the meadow between the table and the stream for meetings. On cold days, a great fire would be kindled.

Farther south first were the tables and cabinets of the men and women who made the wine, that delicious, mind-clouding, tender-making drink. Generations ago—Teller told it as at least seven lifetimes—a container of fruit juice had been left aside in the summer heat for several days. A woman found it, smelled a peculiar sour-sweet aroma, and gave it to her husband to taste. He tasted and drank it down, later roared with laughter, and later still woke with a headache, and wine had been discovered. Calor was the village's winemaker. He had many helpers—and users, who would bring him their products in exchange. He was very popular.

Then the potters! Another dedicated team that made clay pots for the wine and many other objects so useful to the tribe—plates and cups of all kinds, holders of all liquids to be kept or destroyed, and pots with closed lids to store food and everything else worth keeping. They knew where to go along the bank of the Great River to find open slopes of the finest clay to be spun and formed and set out in the sun to dry.

Further down was Artisan's workshop, where he, the man who knew how things worked (and wondered out the things he didn't know,) made tools of wood, bone, and stone and built tables and benches. Near him, the women used his tools to fashion clothing and blankets. The north end of the village was where the carcasses of hunted animals were brought and butchered and food was prepared.

At this end, the stream served for washing clothes and implements, and nearby for bathing, then toilet space.

Over many lifetimes, the village had created itself, from a small family of cold, hungry people to a busy, self-confident settlement with growing skills and developing customs that grew precious with age.

Today was the day after Rest Day, not a Meeting Day (they were held the day before Rest, Market Day), but the elders of the village were at the table, sipping a warm tea of water and herbs.

Present were Elwin, Teller, Abel, Gratia, and Maire. They sat around a smallish table with carved wooden cups. Elwin was a wiry man of medium height with brown hair and a beard turning gray, brown eyes, and a slender, calm face that showed his wrinkles and easily showed a smile or frown. He had been the tribe's leader for thirty years. Teller was his historian, the man responsible for memorizing the tribe's origin and history and producing it on request. Maire sat next to him, a veteran and widow with a level head and a long perspective. Her good friend Abel was Elwin's father and his predecessor as Tribe leader. Gratia was Elwin's wife and the teacher of the village children up to the age of thirteen.

"Hello, Winnie!" Elwin said, "Sit down, have a tea."

"Good morning. I'd love one." Winnie sat and greeted Gratia, who had filled a small bowl when she spotted Winnie coming.

All were dressed in simple animal-skin robes, knee length and without sleeves. "Thanks. You look lovely as usual, Gratia. What's new?"

"Nothing much. In the late day, I'm thinking. We haven't seen Calor yesterday or this morning either. He's usually up and out by now."

"Hmm..." Winnie pursed her lips. "Sure, he'll usually be out with the girls, leading the search for sweet fruits for his wine." She added, "And he's been walking out to see people over at the River Tribe once or twice a Moon—with wine usually. I think he brings some to Ruse or Diss. Trades it, maybe. I don't know what for."

Elwin raised his eyes. "Calor's a prosperous sort, you may have noticed. Best skins and sandals. I'll have a talk with him when he shows up."

And the conversation turned to other things.

3

Calor didn't appear the next morning, either. Elwin and his second-in-command, Teller, walked down to the winery area and sought out Calor's assistant, Eadred. They found him tasting a large pot full of fermenting juice.

"Hi there, Eadred, How's the wine? And where's your boss?" greeted Elwin.

Eadred looked up, a smile on his chronically worried face. "Wine's pretty good. Calor put some crushed seeds in this batch." He stood up and wiped his hands on his robe. "As to Calor, I don't know. Haven't seen him since Market Day, three days ago. He's usually not away that long."

"Where does he go?"

"He usually doesn't say, but he takes Nie with him to carry an extra container or two of wine. And Nie says they go to the River to see Diss. That's nearly a day's travel, as you know. He's back on the second day, sometimes the third, but never more."

"What does he bring back with him?" Teller asked.

"Well, I'm not usually around when he returns."

Teller turned to Elwin. "Let's go over to his tent and talk to Ariola."

Elwin looked upwards, thinking. "Tell you what, Teller. This may raise a lot of questions. Why don't you take Stride, and the two of you start asking around?"

"All right," said Teller. "Stride would be good. Are they out hunting today, do you know?"

"I don't think so. They were out before Market Day, got a good haul. Will you take the job?"

Teller said, "Of course. I'll find the young man." And he cornered Stride up near Winnie's garden. "Hey, Stride, I've got a job for you. A job for us, actually."

Stride turned away from Winnie's herbs, saw Teller, straightened up, and grinned. "Hello, sir. Sure thing. Tell me what." Everybody liked Teller. He was a little schoolteacher-ish sometimes but always friendly and never put on airs. He was tall and full-bodied, with a black beard on a wide-mouthed face.

"No one's seen Calor for a couple of days, and he didn't tell anyone where he was going. Elwin's worried. So you and I have the job of finding him. Let's start by talking to Ariola."

The two of them wandered into the trees and found Calor's tent. It was a handsome one, with good skins and a thatched roof, and plenty of room inside for the two of them and some good wooden furniture. Ariola was at the entrance, looking up at the weather.

"Good day, Ariola," said Teller politely. "Yes, it does look like a storm coming. We're wondering about your husband's whereabouts. May we come in and discuss it?"

"Oh, sure." Ariola looked at them both, then outside again, and gave a nervous smile. "I've been wondering, too."

She sat on the bed. The two men glanced around, then sat on two stout boxes. There were hooks for clothing and a pair of tables for preparing and eating food. She glanced at Teller, then down.

"Did he go off again to the River?"

"I don't know."

"He often does, doesn't he? I suspect he's doing a little wine trading with the River Tribe folks we know."

"Yes, he does."

"When did you see him last? Tell us about it." Teller leaned forward, his face now serious.

"I—I think he went off two or three mornings ago. He took Nie with him; he usually does, to carry things. She cleared her throat. We had an argument that morning. He ended it by just leaving, didn't say why or when he'd be back. Nie had two pots of wine to carry."

Stride glanced at Teller, received a slight nod, and asked, "He usually comes back again by the second evening, doesn't he?"

"Yes. But—he was angry this time."

"Whom does he visit, do you know?"

"Diss and his winemaker, so he says. He comes back with wine or a garment or some food."

Teller nodded. "Well, let's give him the rest of the day. If he's not back by morning, we're going to go and find him. His work here is important. Do you need anything?" She shook her head, again looking down.

"Goodbye, now. Come and tell us if anything new happens." The two men left.

Rain came that afternoon, buckets of it, driving everyone to shelter.

And the chill wind rolled in with it, blowing tents and sleeping bags away, leaving puddles in all the low places. Sunrise was welcomed.

4

Calor was not back by morning.

Teller spoke with Elwin, and he and Stride immediately returned to Calor's tent. They spoke, and Ariola appeared at the flap, now with a serene face and an attractive gown. "Gentlemen, please come in."

Teller said, "Good morning. Since Calor has not returned, it's our obligation to search your tent—for anything that might help us find him."

She nodded and stepped back, and the two men entered and looked around. Teller gestured to Stride, and each began a search; Teller at the bed and Stride on the shelves behind the kitchen table. Stride was a little clumsy; he was not used to handling pots and wooden spoons, but he was thorough. Any items unfamiliar to him went on the table. A drinking pot of a different shape and color. A couple of spoons in a different wood, smaller and rounder. On the floor, he noted a carpet, tightly woven of broad leaves and slender branches.

Teller was at work on the wooden boxes beside the big bed, fastened together with wooden nails and topped with thinner wood decorated with color. Inside were woven clothing items, quite soft, from slender plant stems. A bracelet carved from soft wood and colored with something painted on. All very pretty. Then, in one of the boxes, tall, narrow pots of wine. He lifted the wooden stopper from one of them and sniffed a sweet alcoholic vapor, quite different from village wine.

They stood together with sober faces. "Ariola," said Teller softly, "These things come from the River Tribe, don't they?"

"Yes. Calor brings home little gifts for me. He's such a good man..."

"Do you know who the donor is?"

"No, I don't. I don't go with him."

"Does anyone from there visit you?"

"What? Well... he has brought a guest here, sometimes..."

"Who?"

"Someone called Dolor. Their winemaker, I believe."

"Anyone else?"

"No..."

"Thank you. I'll just take a couple of small things along. We're going down to see them," Teller said. "Goodbye."

5

Teller and Stride set out, walking into the morning sun towards the river. It was the Great River, the Euphrates, which snaked down from the northern mountains, making fruitful all the long valley to the Southern Ocean. A day's brisk walking, but a fine sunny day for it. They always kept an eye out for good stands of edible plants, especially trees of fruits, to report to Winnie on their return.

Stride, walking half a step behind Teller to let him set the pace, asked, "Have you ever had to investigate a thing like this? I'm pretty confused, figuring out what to ask and how to act."

Teller chuckled. "Only a few times. And never with somebody outright missing. Two things. One, people will lie to you with smiling faces if they are hiding something. Some of them are good at it. And, sometimes, the smallest detail may reveal the answer."

They ate bread from their pockets along the way and reached the river at sunset, north of the village where the River Tribe had lived for many fathers' times. It was a familiar place to Teller especially, and they nodded and smiled to acquaintances as they made their way to a spot among the trees and slept.

In the morning, after eating the rest of their bread and washing it down with water from a spring, they made their way to Ruse's tent on a gentle hill right on the west riverbank.

Ruse was the chief of the River Tribe, and under him, it had grown and flourished. His and Adam's Tribe, headed by Elwin, had been friendly for over two hundred summers, growing from casual interactions to a tradition of a Spring Festival at the beginning of the warm season, when in the old days, the tribes would pack up and spend the summer months roaming and hunting. That practice was diminishing now, as more of the people preferred to stay in their permanent villages, and food-gathering could more easily be done from home.

Ruse's tent was fully worthy of a leader's: large, well-walled and thatched, and divided into two big rooms. Ruse took them into the kitchen-and-meetings room and seated them. "It's good to see you, Teller, and to meet you, young Stride. I've watched you grow these ten years; you're quite a man."

Stride smiled and nodded, and Teller started the conversation. "We came, Ruse, because we've missed our winemaker, Calor, for nearly four days now, and we know he visits you often. Has he been here?

"I don't know," Ruse said. He turned to an aide and said, "Go ask Diss or Dolor if they've seen Calor these six days, will you?" Then to the pair, "You know, Calor brings us a bit of his wine every so often, and we give him a bit of ours. He makes a delicious wine, darker than ours—gets different fruits to put in it, I guess, tricks of the trade, you know." Laughing. "Has he given you a taste of ours?"

"No," said Teller, "but I'll ask him for one. I know he brings back some other things, nice things."

Ruse ducked his head. "Well, let's see. We can walk over there, I suppose."

They arose and went out of the tent, Ruse leading them to Diss's tent nearby. Diss wasn't there, and neither was Oh-san, his wife. They continued south to the wine-making area. Dolor was there, supervising three of his assistants (two young men and a girl), cutting up fruits into small pieces and putting them into large wine-making pots with just enough water and a small cupful of mature wine from another pot. An older man was sealing one of the pots with a wood stopper and leaves, ready to put aside in a shelter.

Dolor answered their question cheerfully. "I haven't seen Calor and Nie for, oh, eight or nine days. They didn't come down this Rest Day. And I haven't seen Diss since, uh, yesterday morning it was. He was picking up some things for me to bring up to Adam's Village, probably tomorrow. Any messages for Elwin?"

Ruse grunted. "No. Check with him, though. What are you bringing?"

"Just a pot of wine for Calor, and I'll bring one of his back. And Ariola asked for a couple of our wooden needles."

"All right then. Thanks, Dolor."

"Sure." They left Dolor. Ruse returned to his tent, and Teller and Stride rambled south, keeping near the river, which even this far north of the sea was wide, clear, and beautiful, with a soft swishing voice around the curves. Teller said softly, "What do you think?"

Stride's shoulders went up and down. "Who else is there to ask?"

"Oh-San, of course, if we can find her. Do you know her?

"No, but I know what she looks like. Let's walk down to the food market, then back up on the west side. I guess nobody's going to offer us food and drink."

"Oh, I'll get us something at the market. And we can sleep among the trees again. It's too far to walk back tonight."

They found Oh-San at the market, fetching food and exchanging for some cloth. Teller approached, raising a friendly hand.

"Hello, Oh-San; I'm Teller from Adam's Village. We missed you at your tent a while ago. Calor's missing, and we're getting worried. May we come and talk about it? This is Stride, one of our young hunters."

"Sure," she said. "Nice to meet you. Come, and we'll have a drink."

Oh-San got them seated in Dolor's tent with a small cup of wine. "Calor's a friend of ours. My husband and he trade tips about wine-making—and joke about each others' names being almost the same. Dolor's going down there tomorrow."

Teller asked, "When did you see Calor last?"

"Let me see... he wasn't here last Rest Day, so it must have been the one before that. He comes with Nie to exchange things. And they're going to make some special drinks for the Spring Festival. That's coming soon, next full moon."

Stride looked thoughtful. "Can you think of any reason why he'd go off like this? A special hunt? A quarrel with somebody here?"

"No," she said. "No trouble that I know of. You might ask around the riverbank; he likes to fish with some of the men sometimes. Come, have a little bread and meat."

"You're very kind," said Teller, smiling. "But we have to go and speak to Diss. Come visit us if you're ever in Adam's Village."

Sunset was splashing color across the western sky when the pair entered Diss's tent. His wife, Nadie, a plump, smiling woman, promised them a good supper and started bustling about to prepare it. They sat down with Diss and told of Calor's absence.

Diss was a short, stocky man with graying black hair and beard to match his dark eyes. "It sounds odd," he declared. "The winemakers are very busy this time of year, no time for wandering off. We have seven women out down the river picking fruit and greens for them. Sounds odd."

"It's more than odd; it's worrying," said Teller. "Have you seen him or Nie lately?"

"Nie? Oh, that young fellow that carries his wine for him. No, but I don't see them often. Lots of coming and going. Starting to prep for the festival. River's full, we had rain and some flooding. Lots to do. What's Elwin up to?"

"Oh, he's busy, same as you." And the conversation went nowhere, and they ate and thanked their host and walked outside to sleep in the trees, wrapped in their cloaks.

Stride didn't sleep at once. He walked westward and pondered what he had heard. He was strong and smart, a good hunter, but he had no experience in this sort of thing. Nobody seemed to know anything about Calor or to care much. Could they be on the wrong track? Were they holding back? "Well, I'm getting smarter fast, I guess."

Soon, he spotted a knot of trees, with one long dead trunk among them. He went closer. Yes, there was enough room to slip under the trunk and enough dry leaves for comfort and warmth. Carefully, he gathered the driest leaves and pushed them under the trunk, more at one end. Then he wiggled his body atop the leaves, turned on his side, pulled some leaves up around his shoulders, then his robe, and settled comfortably into sleep.

6

In the cool breezy morning, Stride and Teller discussed their frustration and planned their day. "I'm about out of ideas," grumbled Teller. "Maybe we should just walk home and check with Elwin; maybe Calor's back."

Stride looked up, then waved an arm. "Nie! Over here!" Teller looked too, and there was Nie, by himself, walking through the trees. Nie looked up, saw his fellow Adam villagers, and turned to join them.

"We're delighted to see you, young man," cried Teller, clapping Nie's shoulder with a strong hand. "We've been looking for Calor these four days and no trace of him. Will you fill us in?"

They found a place where all three could sit, and Teller started in. "Nie, just tell us where *you've* been since last Market Day. Will you?"

"Calor and I came across to the River on Market Day last, the day before Rest Day. I gave him the wine I'd carried and spent the evening with friends. I could have come home on Rest Day—I didn't see Calor—but I stayed in River. I saw Dolor. He asked me to bring another pot back to River during the week—Calor's orders, he said. Next morning, I walked back to Adam with the gifts from Dolor that Calor had given me. I gave them to Ariola for safe keeping, and then I came back here with the wine Dolor asked for. Calor wasn't back when I left; I haven't seen him since Market Day evening."

Stride asked, "Who else did you play with here on Rest Day?"

Here Nie showed signs of nervousness. He turned his head and looked away. Then he cleared his throat and said, "I've got a girlfriend here. I stayed with her Rest Day night, and I'm staying with her now." He looked down.

"I think we need to have a chat with her," said Teller. "Do you want to tell her about us and prepare her to talk? We'll be nearby."

"Okay." Nie stood up and walked away northward.

Stride looked at Teller. "I think we're starting to hear a slightly different story."

Teller leaned forward and back, as he was likely to do when excited. "I think so too. Let's keep it a secret for now. We'll have to see a few people again."

River people were beginning to glance at them as they passed by. They walked to the riverbank and up and down, just casually. It wasn't long before Nie found them again. "Come," he said, "she's ready."

Layla had a small but tidy tent—stout sticks with a thatched roof. They sat on the ground in front of the tent flap. She was a young, slender girl with yellow hair tied back halfway down the waist. Her face was fair, with brown eyes and a definite chin, and her attitude was friendly and confident. "Good morning," she said. "It's nice to meet friends of Nie and Calor."

"Thank you for meeting with us, Layla. Our mutual friend Calor seems to have gone off somewhere, and we need him back at our winery. As a friend, would you just tell us about your activities since a day or two before last Rest Day, and what you know about his movements?"

"I'll do my best." She stared at nothing for ten seconds but comfortably.

"I often see Calor and Nie when they come to trade wine. I saw them both last Market Day, in the evening. Calor went directly to Dolor with his wine and things. I talked with Nie until he returned, then Dolor and I came here to eat and you,

Nie, went off to eat with friends. Calor left pretty early in the morning of Rest Day, I think to walk back to Adam. Later, Nie and his friends stopped by, and we had a drink, and Nie stayed the night with me and left—that would be the morning after Rest Day—with wine and gifts from Dolor to bring home. Does that cover it.?"

Stride gave her an appraising look and a careful smile. "I should think that covered it very well."

Teller picked right up. "Just a few clarifications. Did you see Calor on Rest Day morning?"

"Ah, no. He was gone when I awakened."

"All right. From his mood and conversation, did you notice anything that might explain his disappearance?

"No. He seemed perfectly normal to me."

"Do you know of any problems or differences with anyone here that might play a role?"

Layla frowned. "That's a harder question. Calor and Dolor had a complicated arrangement—of trading not only wine but other useful things—clothing and tools. They gave and received things from people here, including important people. Of course, I was never directly involved, never witnessed these things. I just heard Dolor talk about them, mostly."

"Tell me about any problems if you can."

"As Dolor told it, the arrangement just sort of happened. Calor started it by bringing some wine and wanting Dolor to give it to Diss and Ruse, just out of friendship. That was years ago. The wine was liked, and Dolor started to offer things in exchange—furniture and tools for the men and clothing and decoration for the women. They kept it pretty quiet from the leaders; Diss knew about it in general. Ruse was kept out of it. And on the Adam end, I only know that gifts were never offered to you (bowing to Teller) or Elwin or the other elders. It was pretty much for Calor and his wife, as far as I know."

"Did Diss ever ask Dolor for inside information on Elwin, tribal matters?"

"You're way beyond what I know." Layla lifted her chin ,smiled at Teller, and shared it with Stride, too. "They never talked that way with me around."

Stride smiled back, a sort of half smile. "You did get around, though, didn't you?"

Layla said smugly, "Pretty well, pretty well."

Teller was pressing his fingers together, thinking. "So Layla, just one more question. In your conversations, what—unfriendly—things were said about Calor?

"Oh, nothing more that I can think of."

"Well, thank you for trying to help us. I'm still baffled."

The two got up, bowed to Layla, and began to walk back toward the riverbank. Suddenly, they heard the sound of voices and saw a group of men coming up from the south. They hastened toward the voices and heard, "...dead. We fished his body out of the river." They got close enough to see Laeso, Dolor's assistant.

"Who?"

"Dolor. They've got him down there."

Stride and Teller rushed down the path, brushing others aside. A few hundred yards away, four men were carrying the corpse on a makeshift litter. Teller approached, and since he was older and carried himself with authority, when he asked, "Please. Let me see him," the men stopped and lay their burden down on the grass. It was Dolor's body, naked, cold, and gray. His skull and face were crushed as by multiple blows from a heavy object. Stride goggled while Teller looked carefully at the body. He picked up an arm. It was soft and flaccid. The skin was pockmarked with small bites and was darker on the back. But the face and eyes were still visible. Teller looked up.

"He's been in the water a few days. Probably not drowned, dead when he hit the water. No signs I could see of struggle, just the blows to the head that killed him." He turned to the men. "Thank you, carry on." To Stride, he said, "Let's get out of here."

They walked back to Layla's tent, and she was there. "Layla," Teller said gently, "That was Dolor. He's been killed. We're going to walk back to our village, and I advise you to come with us."

"Let me think," she said.

"You've exposed their lies."

He turned to Stride. "Can you find Nie and bring him here? I think we all need to go. I am going to tell Ruse."

He walked back to Ruse's tent, announced himself to the assistant, and waited. Ruse appeared.

"Have you heard that Dolor is dead?"

"Just this minute. I can tell you nothing now."

"Of course. It is my duty to return and inform Elwin. We will need to investigate this tragedy and Calor's disappearance together. I will take with me Stride, Nie, and Nie's friend. Do you have any message for Elwin?"

"Just that I agree with you."

"Farewell." *And*, he thought to himself, *let's get out of here.*

7

Teller was thinking and remembering. He knew about tragedy. When he was seven, there had been a very bad storm. It was spring, and the family was near the river, making and mending for the summer trek. The small boys had no duties and were just fooling around, throwing stones at the water and making them skip.

"Three!" cried Teller as his round, flat stone hit the surface beautifully and skidded away. Stane threw his too hard; it rose and plunged with no skips. "The wind took it," he complained. The wind was now gusting.

Goswhit was older and strong; he threw his with a low, sweeping sidearm. Three, four, five bounces. "I win!"

They all scrambled around looking for good flat stones. The wind was colder now and stronger; it began shaking the trees. A blinding bolt of lightning struck the ground fifty feet away. Teller could feel the hair rise on his head. Goswhit ran toward the tree on an upslope to have a look.

He stared out across the water, then turned and screamed, "Spinner! Get down!" Men took up the cry; mothers hurried the children toward the trees. There was no time to hide. A huge gray shape roared toward them across the water, spinning.

Teller hung onto his tree as the terrible wind pulled at him and sent stones flying into his face. He would never forget the roar. The tree next to him was pulled out of the earth roots and all and went flying away with Goswhit hanging on blindly. A stone struck Teller's knee, which twisted and bled. He held on.

The next day, the men dug a grave and buried Goswhit. His mother wept. The family head, Abel, praised him while they all stood around the grave.

"The world has taken him," he said. "Perhaps the Maker will keep his spirit."

That was that, and Teller pondered many times on those words, wondering about death and life. He kept a limp the rest of his life and treasured all the stories he learned as he trained to be the tribe's historian.

Now he had another death to wonder about and remember.

8

It was a long and mostly silent walk back to Adam. Everyone wanted to put off talking about what had happened, each for his or her own reasons. They arrived after dark. Teller made room for Layla to sleep in his tent and to break fast with him in the morning. She recognized her dangerous position and was content to wait passively.

In the morning, Teller and Stride briefed Elwin and the other listeners—Gratia, Abel, and Maire.

Teller began with a summary of the last three days' happenings with the River Tribe, starting with Calor's still unsolved vanishing and ending with the discovery of Dolor's body, an obvious murder victim.

Then he said, "Now, I want to go over the points where the stories Stride and I heard contradict each other or the facts, in my opinion. I'm your historian, and you know that I've cultivated the knack of remembering very accurately what I hear. So here are the things I wonder about:

1) Ruse, Diss, Dolor, and Oh-San didn't see Calor on Market Day, but Nie and Layla did.

2) Neither Layla nor Nie saw Calor on the morning of Rest Day, although she apparently slept with him the previous night, and Nie was there the next morning. Did Calor disappear during the night?

3) His wife, Ariola, had an argument with him before (as she confirms) he left for the River on Market Day morning. But she has no clue who might have been angry with him, or whom all the presents were for. Is she hiding something?

4) Ruse knows absolutely no details about the winemakers' complicated deal—and I believe him—he was kept from those details. Diss also knows no details, and that I don't believe. He both gave to and received valuables from Dolor.

And so, I am suspicious that Calor's disappearance is tied up with Dolor's death. Calor, too, may have been killed. That's probable now. And we are all planning to have a joyous Spring Festival with the River Tribe in less than a moon. What shall we do?"

There was a long silence at the table.

Finally, Elwin spoke. "Teller, Stride. We thank you most heartily for the search you have undertaken and the results you have obtained. We are faced with a situation we have never experienced before—an apparent killing of one of our number and the chilling of our relationship with a tribe we have long considered friends. It's bad news. But you've dug up enough evidence to warn us in time.

"What do we do when human evil strikes our tribe? Well, we look to our traditions. What actions do we consider proper, even necessary, to stop the evil—I guess I should call it crime—and to punish the people responsible for it?"

He looked around the table.

Gratia spoke. "If the crime is contained within a family, we have sometimes left the punishment to the head of that family."

Abel responded, "Yes, if the trouble hasn't spread to others, that's a good thing to do. The family is precious, older than the tribe, and its strength should be protected."

And Teller continued, "And if the origin is outside the tribe, we can bring our hurt to their leadership and give them responsibility for correcting it."

Elwin nodded. "Also a good choice if our relations are good and the tribe shares our view of crime and punishment. It would be like having a common rule that covers us both. I'd like to work that way with the River Tribe—if we trust them to act properly."

Maire put up a finger. "That method depends on the severity of the crime. I'd be quite confident that Ruse could deal with something like theft. We've seen or heard about punishments such as requiring extra work, taking away property, even exile. But with killing—I don't know."

It was Elwin's turn again. "Let's talk about that. What is the just punishment for killing? The just range of punishments, depending on the circumstances of the act. Killing the guilty person is the extreme. The other actions Maire mentions are possible. Let the punishment fit the crime. But is death ever the answer? I'd like to hear from all of you."

The Listeners glanced at one another, looked forward, tapped fingers on wood.

Abel started. "I say yes. But here's what I'd do.First, be sure we have the guilty person. Then confront him—or her—and let them speak in their own defense. Then consider character, circumstances, the likelihood of repeating the crime, and take a vote on it."

Maire said, "That was good. I agree."

Gratia paused. "I'm not certain. I guess I would look carefully for another option—that would protect us and save a life—and if none is found, I would agree to death."

Teller said, "I agree."

Elwin said, "So we agree. In this situation, we are still at the beginning. We don't know if Calor was killed, and if so, who killed him. I shall consult with Teller and Stride and plan two things: a thorough search for Calor and a meeting with Ruse."

"We'll break up now and reconvene tomorrow to review what we will say to Ruse when we meet him—the whole Council—in two days. Teller and Stride, please stay behind."

When the others had filed out, Elwin said to Teller and Stride, "I'm going to ask you two, plus another of your choice for added security, to stand ready to return to River and clear the way with Ruse for me to visit. That means that the search party for Calor will need a different leader. Who do you think I should appoint?

"Well...," said Teller, "someone who knows our villagers well and has the authority to command their obedience. Hunter, I think. In fact, he can gather his hunters quickly to constitute an excellent search party."

"Perfect," Elwin said. "Stride, you're one of his trusted men; will you talk to him?"

Stride nodded and got to his feet. "I'll find him right now. We can talk over how to conduct the search and come back to you today for approval."

"Fine. I know it's Market Day, but I'd like the search party to start out tomorrow before sunrise. Now, for you two. I want you to go back and talk to Ruse tomorrow. Tell him that we have a joint problem with criminal behavior. We don't know who's responsible, but it's pretty obvious that the actions of both our winemakers have led to it, and it has to stop. Ask for his support of our search party and to be ready for a visit from me and my council the day after tomorrow to agree on actions to find and punish the guilty and end the problem. How does that sound?"

Stride and Teller agreed, and went off to execute the plan.

9

At sunup the next morning, Hunter and twenty men and women were going on a hunt. But instead of animals for meat and hides, their object was to find signs of, or the body of, Calor, the village winemaker.

It was late spring, the days were getting long, the weather cool and dry. The course would take them in a circle around Adam's Village, then on a long march just south of east all the way to the Euphrates River. They knew the route well; it was trodden frequently between the two friendly tribes; there were even visible paths part of the way. First forest, then open fields; then open woods leading to the River Tribe's village.

They were armed, but not with the weapons of hunting. There were long walking sticks, ropes, and wooden shovels, as well as food and water for them, and hides on a branch-made sledge in case a body needed to be carried. One or two had serious hunting weapons: clubs of wood and wooden knives with the hardwood blades sharpened on sandstone or flint. Two women carried food and water; one of them had bandages and potions for wounds. They set out briskly in the dawn grayness, singing an old marching song:

To the darkness in the forest breathes the grayness of the light
When the melodies of morning stun the silence of the night
There's a rustle in the grasses and a trickle in the brook

The great Sun turns to stare at us whose face forbids our look.
Glory, glory to the morning
And welcome to the day.

They walked north along the stream a little way. Then Hunter extended his hands. The men moved silently out to the right and left, ten feet or so apart. The right column was led by Stride, the left by an older man, Hawk. When all were spread out, Hunter gave a forward motion with his arms, and the men started forward in a broad circle to the right, intent on the ground before them and the trees above, searching for any sign of human passage. Silence prevailed, broken only by quiet remarks and pointed fingers.

Nothing suspicious was found in the circle around their village, and Hunter stopped and wheeled the rows of men around to the left until he was facing a little south of east. Then forward again, slower than a march but not as silent, and they set out for the river.

Hours before, in the dark, Teller and Stride had set forth on the same course. They wanted to give Ruse and his advisors most of the day to search for evidence and get ready to meet Elwin. They wondered aloud what attitude Ruse would take—casual, downplaying the extent of the trouble; hostile, ready to shift the blame to the absent Calor; or friendly and cooperative. You never knew with Ruse; he was a man of moods. They'd brought Rubor along with them: Calor's cousin, tall and muscular, casually armed with a club. A good man to have along in a fight.

Maybe they'd need him. They reached the outskirts of the River Village with the sun high above the trees and were turning to head for Ruse's tent when they were surrounded by soldiers out of nowhere, armed and helmeted. "Stop, strangers!"

Teller calmly introduced themselves and asked for an escort to Ruse. The soldiers told them to stay where they stood while one of them ran off for orders. He soon returned, and Adam's men were hustled to Ruse's tent without incident.

Back at the Adam Council table, Elwin was briefing his colleagues on the meeting with Ruse tomorrow.

"Why are we going there?" Abel complained. "They should be coming to us."

"Maybe so," replied Elwin. "It's just that we're moving more quickly than they seem to be. And so far, it's their winemaker who's been murdered. But I know what you mean." He continued, "Our approach will depend a lot on whether the search team finds Calor or evidence of him. They're on their way east now. Teller will meet them tonight, and he'll send Stride back early to meet us on the way.

Stride can report on the search and tell us what Ruse's attitude is before we meet.

Gratia sighed. "That makes it really hard to take a position."

Elwin said, "You're sure right on that one. But let's review what we know and what's at stake.

"We know our winemakers—both of them—were cheating on us for profit.

We know their winemaker is dead, murdered, and we suspect ours is, too.

We know that some of their stories are...improbable. Diss must know more than he's telling us. Oh-San too. Will they open up now that murder has been committed? Why should they? Because the whole relationship between us is endangered. If it has value, we've got to regain trust before the Spring Festival."

Maire said, "Yes, all of that. Do <u>we</u> have any additional tales to tell? What about Ariola? What about Eadred?"

"You're right. We need to question both of them again. Shall we do it now, together? Or one on one? Which would get us farther?

"Together," said Abel. "We need to scare them, impress them with how big this is."

Elwin looked each person in the eye, slowly, then said, "Objections? No. Gratia and Maire, will you call Ariola first?"

Ariola sat at the council table, facing the members. She looked smaller, shoulders together, her face haggard.

Elwin spoke. "Ariola, we share your fears about Calor. We have a search party out, looking for signs of him all the way to the river. The winemaker of the River Tribe was killed by someone. To protect our tribe, it's necessary to know all we can about the barter activities between your husband and members of the River Tribe—especially Dolor."

Ariola looked up at him. "He made advances to me when Calor was away. I didn't tell Calor right away. I should have. I hated Dolor."

Elwin paused and glanced at Gratia. Then he continued. "Please tell us about your last contact with Dolor."

"He was here three days before last Market Day, oh—nine, ten days ago. He brought gifts. Yes, he touched me then. Next day, he left, and that evening, Calor returned. He'd crossed paths with Dolor on the way. He said nothing that night, but next morning, he was angry and demanded to know what Dolor was doing, sneaking here when he was gone. I told him Dolor tried to touch me, that I hated him. He was quiet and stiff the rest of the day. On the next day, Market Day, he picked up Nie and some wine and left to go back east. That's the last I saw of either of them."

In the silence, Elwin nodded to Gratia, who stood up, went to Ariola, and escorted her away.

Abel also traded nods with Elwin; he went after Eadred and returned with him in about a quarter of an hour. Eadred was a stocky redhead with a ready smile concealed by his long beard. This was his story:

"Calor began asking for extra pots of wine last Harvest Moon. He would give the fruit pickers a little something for their extra work. And he started traveling to the river. The number of extra pots grew to two or three a week this moon. But he never asked me to help with moving them or anything about gifts. He did give me an extra pot of wine every moon as his assistant. I never went with him to the River Tribe. I did encounter Dolor a few times around here. The last time was about ten days ago."

Eadred was thanked and dismissed. Elwin asked for thoughts. Maire said, "I suppose we must be honest with the River people about how Dolor acted with Ariola and that Calor was probably angry with him."

Elwin said, "Yes, we must. It's just one of the things that might have led to the violence. Well, we'll stop now. Get ready for the trek tomorrow; we should leave at early dawn."

10

It was the middle of another bright, breezy spring day when Elwin, Maire, Abel, and Gratia climbed to the top of an open slope and stared eastward. The path ahead was gently downhill, grassy, with trees in the distance. And small in that distance were the figures of Teller, Stride, Rubor, and another man coming toward them.

Soon, they were sitting together under one of the trees, munching food and passing around a skin of water Stride had brought. Elwin said, "All right, Teller. Give us the news."

"They didn't find Calor," said Teller. "Tell them about it." The fourth man was Hawk, who had been a leader on the Search team. "We did a careful search around the outside of our village and then right down the common path to the river. We spread out twenty men as far as we could still to see objects or broken ground. Nothing was buried there, and we saw no objects or clues. Of course, we covered only a bit of all this ground—" he waved his hands "—but it would take an assailant time to move a body far enough to the side, and there wasn't much time if Calor was attacked that Market Day night. Also, we didn't have time to walk the river up and down very far, especially not on the far side. He's somewhere, but we don't know where." He shrugged with his hands palms up. "The men took a southern path home, and they'll keep looking on the way."

"Thanks to them all for a right good job," said Elwin. "Now, how are Ruse and Diss taking all this? What's their attitude?"

"I'm not sure," said Teller. "Let me just narrate a bit. We came into Ruse's tent yesterday, escorted by guards. There was an air of militance about the place—solemn faces, people hurrying in and out—it was the opposite of relaxed. They were taking it seriously. But when we entered Ruse's room, he greeted us cordially —not casually, but he wasn't hostile either, just sober.

"I said that the killing of Dolor and the vanishing of Calor were both tragedies, were probably rooted in their wine trading activities, and may have involved crimes on both sides. That we had heard incomplete stories in our questioning and hoped that more frankness would result in more understanding. And finally, that we, too, would have more information from our witnesses in Adam's Village and that we wanted to proceed as a common court in finding and correcting the crimes.

His response was that he agreed and that he thought we would be able to work through this crisis and retain our friendship. He recommends that he and Diss meet with your council briefly today, then after a meal and rest, commence a formal investigation tomorrow morning.

"I cannot tell what he intends."

The council members nodded, and Elwin said, "Our thanks to you three. You have walked into a threatening situation and have obtained the kind of mutual understanding we need in order to proceed. You've stated our position without overstating it. Let's agree and proceed toward the 'preliminary meeting' they wish to give us this afternoon. I'll try to use it to make tomorrow easier and maybe more productive."

Abel asked, "Did he give you any more information on Dolor's death?"

Teller responded, "No, and I didn't ask. I wanted you all here to hear it."

The group now merged and walked eastward. Ruse had provided a tent and surrounding area sufficient for the Adam group to rest and spend the night, and they proceeded there. Thirst quenched and refreshed, they were escorted to Ruse's tent. He was there with Diss and two other leaders, who, after greetings, sat in a row opposite the entrance. Benches were set up facing them, and Rubor, Stride, Teller, Elwin, Gratia, Abel, and Maire sat in that order. (Elwin had brought along a young man and woman to help with carrying and so forth; they were left outside.)

Ruse spoke first. "Welcome, leaders from Adam's Tribe. We and you have carried on a friendship for many lifetimes; never has it been so seriously tested. We were too trustful. We have allowed the friendly exchange of wine between our two winemakers to develop into a serious matter of trading wine for valuable goods without the openness and oversight we should have given it. Evidently, disagreements and jealousies arose. Your winemaker is missing. Ours was killed, murdered. And now we look at one another with a lack of trust. How can we restore trust and confirm our friendship?" He moved a hand toward Elwin.

Elwin said, "You have stated the case well, Ruse. I would like to tell you of the additional information we have from interviews with our people.

"We questioned Ariola, Calor's wife. She, of course, knew of the wine trading and was often the recipient of goods given to her husband in exchange—clothing, jewelry, furniture, tools. Some of these may have been passed along to others; we don't know yet. No council members have received any of the items.

"Ariola told us two things which you must know. First, that she had been approached and touched by Dolor, who wanted her sexual favors. Second, that this had been discovered by Calor and resulted in a serious argument between him and Ariola. The result was his hasty departure back to the river on the Market Day nine days ago. He disappeared that night and has not been found. A search party has just concluded a search for him or clues to him from our village to yours but with no result.

"We also questioned Eadred, Calor's assistant winemaker. He was aware of the increased wine production and witnessed the carrying of wine by Calor or Nie (a young helper) away, presumably to your village. He did not receive any gifts from your village, only a pot of wine every moon for his extra work.

"That's all we've found out so far. But as you know, Teller, with Stride's help," each man raised his hand briefly, "talked to some of you about this matter, and he has a few observations to make. Teller?"

Teller cleared his throat. "I questioned you, Ruse, and you, Diss, briefly, hoping to find news of Calor. I also questioned Dolor himself before he was killed, his wife Oh-San, and a young lady, Layla, a particular friend of young Nie. Here is what I found:

"Ruse, Diss, Dolor, and Oh-San said they didn't see Calor on Market Day—but he was there, and Nie and Layla did. And Diss, I was told that you and Dolor actively traded wine for goods.

"Neither Layla nor Nie saw Calor on the morning of Rest Day—although she apparently slept with him the previous night, and Nie was there the next morning. Did Calor disappear during the night?

"I believe that, before Dolor's death, I was told less than some of you knew about the troubles. We need to hear the rest."

Diss had frowned when Layla's name was mentioned.

11

The next morning, Ruse had asked for two hours for internal discussion before the meeting, and this was readily granted. So it was mid-morning. The warm south wind had brought clouds from the east, and now they covered most of the sky.

The participants took the same places as yesterday. As Ruse had asked, a few other people had been admitted, either as spectators or potential witnesses, and they stood along the side walls—Oh-San, Layla, Laeso, the man who found Dolor's body, two River guards, and Hawk.

When all were in place, Ruse raised his hands, and conversation ceased. He said, "Let's agree that the statements we made and heard yesterday are known and need not be repeated. I would like to call a few witnesses in response to Teller's questioning of earlier statements made to him. Oh-San?"

Oh-San stood and moved to face Ruse, her back to the Adam councilors. Ruse asked, "We are trying to place Calor in the days before his disappearance. Are you certain you did not see him on Market Day nine days ago?"

Oh-San had been told she would be questioned, and she answered without hesitation, "I did not see him. I was keeping to myself that day in case Dolor needed help."

"Did you see him the day before or the day after?"

"No."

Ruse said, "Thank you, Oh-San. The Court grieves with you. You may go."

Oh-San retreated from before Ruse but stayed in the room.

Ruse said, "I testify that I did not see him either, on any of those three days. Now, Diss, I am going to ask you the same question. You don't have to get up."

Diss gave Teller a steely look, then turned his eyes to Ruse. "On reflection, I did see Calor on that Market Day. He was with his young assistant, and Dolor brought me a pot of his wine. I didn't speak with Calor."

Diss now hesitated, then waved a hand at Ruse, cleared his throat, and spoke again.

"Teller, about your impression that I helped Dolor in his exchange of wine for goods. I did. I was of the opinion that barter between the Tribes was a good thing. I still think that. But I accept responsibility for not being more involved. I should have developed rules for openly and fairly trading. I don't know whether I could have prevented the personal missteps that led these people into jealousy and even killing."

There was a quiet collective gasp at Diss's statement.

Now Elwin spoke. "Serious problems require serious solutions. For our part, I promise two things. First, that I will engage with you to create those open rules for barter and see that they are obeyed. Second, that if Calor is found alive, he and his wife, Ariola, will be banished from this Tribe."

Ruse answered, "And I will respond in kind. I will, with Elwin, make and obey new rules. And Diss and I have agreed that he will leave the River Tribe."

The gasp was greater. The leaders gave it a couple of minutes to settle in, and then Ruse said, "I believe we can end this meeting. Elwin, let's work together to have a great Spring Festival. We haven't much time!"

The two stood and clasped arms, and the meeting became a melee and flowed out into the gathering clouds.

12

Everyone was back home, and the council was holding a weekly meeting. Elwin had reviewed the difficult week of searching for Calor. He described seeing the distrust arise between the tribes and its solution in Calor's presumed death and Diss's self-exile.

"You will have noticed something—something painful and worrying. Neither man's killer has been found. I decided that the agreement on punishment (an unspoken conviction of Diss) was enough to settle our dispute. But of course, we'll keep searching for Calor or his fate.

Then, with relief, he went over the schedule for the Spring Festival.

"One more thing: last year, a few of you declined to go on the summer journey; you said that it was nowadays too inconvenient to uproot your families and bring your comforts. We understand. Just tell us, in the next seven days, who chooses to stay."

Finally, there was a meeting of the Naming Committee, when anyone could bring or describe a new discovery that didn't have a name.

Winnie had an item. "Here's a strange little fellow," she said, spreading out a plant on the table so everyone could see it. The stem had pointed leaves and some beautiful white flowers, but the main attraction was the root. Instead of a normal, skinny root, this one was distended into an oblong mass as big as a boy's clenched hand, colored a handsome reddish brown.

"It looks like a potato, of course," she said, "but it's not." Using a sharp wooden knife, she sliced the root expertly down its center. The interior was much the color of the skin, only shinier. "And it tastes delicious boiled." Small slices were cut off for each to taste.

"Mmm, like honey almost," said Gratia. "What should we name it?"

Winnie said, "A sweet potato, I think. I'll try to find a bed of them next week."

Abel said, "All agreed?" Nods. "Done. Any other items?"

A boy who'd been quietly listening raised his hand. "I've got something," he said. "I found it growing near the stream, down that way." He pointed south. "Look." He held up a shiny, green object nearly as big as his head, rounded like an elongated ball.

"Let me see, Tim," said Winnie. She took the object, felt around it, smelled it, held it up to the sun, and tapped it with her fingers—it gave a muffled thump in return. "It's a fruit of some kind. I haven't seen one this big. Shall we open it?"

Abel agreed and produced a wooden knife. Winnie set it on the table and cut it in half. It had a moist, crisp pink interior. Juice trickled onto the table. "It smells sweet," she said and used the knife to cut off a tiny piece, which she touched with her tongue, waited, then swallowed. "Very good." Slices were cut for all the judges and the boy. "What is it?" he said, biting into his slice.

"Let's call it a Mellow," Winnie said. "A Green Mellow, to mark it, in case a different kind shows up." And to the boy, "Tomorrow you have to show me where you found it."

"Oh yes!" And the meeting ended with smiles and dripping fingers.

Gratia gathered her pupils, the village's younger children, for a lesson. She had been teaching youngsters for decades, and there was no one in the village who didn't love her. There were seven of them today, four girls and three boys, aged between three and twelve.

"Today, we'll talk about the weather." She pointed her finger at the oldest girl, Mara. "What does 'weather' mean, dear?"

Mara said stoutly, "If it rains." Gratia smiled. "Well, that's part of it. Who knows what the other parts are?"

Hands went up. Sochi, ten, said, "And snows, sometimes." Glori chimed in, "And hot and cold."

"Very good. And I know you older ones have noticed some other things: In the last Moon, has it gotten colder or warmer?"

"Warmer!" was the general shout.

"Yes! And another thing, in the same time, has the sun come up in the morning earlier or later?

"Earlier!"

And are those two things connected or not—earlier and warmer?"

Young minds were thinking. Mara said, "Well, it usually gets warm when the sun comes up. And things turn green."

Gratia raised up her arms. "That's wonderful, Mara! You've connected those things together! And we think it's because the Sun is very hot—you can just close your eyes and FEEL its hotness, can't you? And so it makes the wind and the ground warm too, and the flowers start to grow. That's called 'cause and effect.' The sun is the cause—you could call it the because—and the warm-ness is the effect. It's warm because the sun is shining. To understand things, always try to see what causes something else—makes it happen."

Aaron, a thoughtful twelve-year-old already beginning his growth spurt, raised his hand.

"Yes, Aaron?"

"Well, I was just wondering. If the sun causes it to get warm, what causes the sun to be so hot?"

Gratia raised her eyebrows then gave Aaron a big smile. "Aaron, that's one of the best questions I have ever heard! It's great because that's got to have a cause, and we don't know what it is. There are a thousand things we don't know yet. You children can help us find them out!

Sochi said, "Lessons cause me to be hungry." And he got laughter from the class.

Gratia stood up and said, "Let's have a song and dance! All the children stood. Gratia raised her arms, then brought them down to start the dance to the well-known verse:

"Pippety-poppity purple and pink!
Brighten and whiten and tighten and blink!
Slicker and quicker and swirl it around
Fizzily dizzily feet on the ground!

Soon, the puffing, happy class was dismissed.

13

Villagers were gradually developing an informal Barter system to get the things they needed. Winnie accepts food or drink for her herbs, often days later, after the illness is better. Likewise, potters trade their pots, weavers their clothes, artisans the things they fashioned. Sometimes on a summer day before the day of rest, the clearing east of the big council table would turn into a regular market, items coming in and out of baskets and agreements being made.

But sometimes, someone would forget to "pay" for what was received, and relations would sour. Then the issue would be brought to the council. The value of the given and received would be discussed; what was a new clay pot worth in return for leaves chewed to calm a stomach? Elwin would say, "It's worth what you agreed it to be worth; how can you say better than that?" and usually that would settle the matter. The council discussed the whole thing.

Elwin said, "Everyone values their own stuff highly."

Maire chuckled. "Yes, and some have less to offer. Just the collections of veggies; some bring in gorgeous piles of fruits and grains, others nothing but leaves and stalks."

Hunter nodded. "My team comes back from a hunt sometimes with more fresh meat than we can carry; other times, just a few birds and squirrels. What we get in return depends on how hungry the cooks are." He chuckled. "Which cook do you go to with the best stuff?"

Elwin said, "Artisan suggested once that we assign pots a value and trade them for everything else."

Teller raised his eyebrows. "Oh, what a complicated mess that would be!"

Abel responded thoughtfully, "Well, not necessarily. You'd have to just value everything else in pots: an armful of apples would be half a pot, a clean and softened antelope hide three pots, a wooden spear five pots, and so forth. And it wouldn't have to be pots. It could be an armful of firewood or something else basic that everyone needs."

Teller said, "Yes, but could you value everything? And, you know, an excellent hide would be worth twice a poor one. And so would a good pot."

Abel said, "Well, you'd have to just value certain basic things in pots to give everyone an idea of what a pot is worth."

Elwin laughed, "The pottery makers would just love that."

Teller replied, "And we'd need a new Historian to keep track of it all. I certainly don't want that job."

Elwin smiled. "Yes, you just keep on remembering our history. But someday, we'll have to figure out a way to keep track of numbers. Art, will you get the right people together and see if a pot system might work? Or something else as a standard? Bread, maybe?"

Art grinned and rubbed his hands together. "I'd love to. Some of the youngsters have been tossing ideas around. I'll get Winnie to be my partner, and we'll ask all the other producers what they think."

Art cornered Winnie in her herb garden and explained the idea. "We want to make bartering—exchanging the things we make with what others make and we need—more fair and sort of standard. Abel thought picking out something to be the basic trade thing, like a pot, and somehow agree that other things would be valued in pots. You know—a handful of herbs, half a pot; a skin of wine, two pots; a scraped and softened deer skin, ten pots, and so forth."

"Goodness!" cried Winnie. "What a new sort of idea! Complicated, though. It would depend on how badly you needed the item, how long it took to make it, how nice it was...."

"Just so," said Art. "And you, my dear lady, are the best possible partner for me to put the ideas together. You understood the concept right away. You're fair; everybody knows that. And you have a good head for value. I...."

Winnie blushed a little. "Such praise! Tell me what you want to do, and we'll do it!"

Art blushed a little, too—a rare thing for him. "We'll make a list, suggest a *range* of values for each item, just to start with—like, the wine could be worth from half a pot to five pots—and then talk to people and get lots of votes on the values. And see how people like the idea."

She said, with a sly smile, "How do you 'make a list'?"

"Yeah, that's the first problem. But listen, here's an idea. I could take a sheepskin and some blacking and make a kind of picture of how a tool looks so that someone else could make one. How about that?"

"Wow."

***

A week later at the council, Art reported back that there was real interest in a barter system.

"Here's the situation as I see it," said Elwin. "We've grown big enough to have groups, which produce different things for the tribe. Each group has things they use as barter. The hunters provide our meat and want it to be worth exchanging for firewood, grains, wine, clothing, and herbs. The winemakers will give us wine in exchange. The herb gatherers provide medicine and greens to eat and for seasoning the food. All those exchanges take place, but it gets complicated—and what's the value of what we exchange? What's worth more than what else?"

"Yes," Teller looked thoughtful. "People want their contributions to be valued, but you and I will differ on what we think it's worth. Should a skin of wine bring a meal of meat, or an armful of wood, or what?"

"Or," said Maeve, "should we just continue to let it be decided by each one? There's something to be said for the freedom to bargain."

"But we also want to know what other people value their coin at—what's the range of values for a bundle of herbs," Teller submitted.

"Well, there is." Maeve frowned. "Trades happen every day, but a lot of us trade on the Market Day, when there's less routine work. I think we should declare Market Day to be Barter Day, encourage people to trade then, and we'd hear all the action."

Abel smiled. "Might even turn into a sort of game - who's willing to give more for what you have up."

"Just so!" Elwin exclaimed. "That might be roaring fun. But we can't let it get out of hand. There ought to be limits everybody knows. Food's not a game."

"Yes, and that's our job, the council's," Abel replied.

"But how do we tell everyone?" Teller was getting excited. "We need some kind of public board—a place where we can put up the values for everybody to see, and it's our responsibility to see that the values are about right."

"Whoa," said Abel, smiling. "We're getting into deep woods here. But suppose... suppose we pick out a basic thing we all need, that's easy to make or find, and give it a value of 'One.' Like maybe a length of good twine as long as a man, or a piece of firewood.

"What about a chunk of bread?" cried Maeve. "Everybody wants that."

"Sure, or bread. Then everything else will get a value of equal to or more than one—two for a piece of cloth the size of your hand, four for enough meat to feed your family, eight for the wine, whatever!"

"Not a single value," said Teller, who was really getting into the (non) game. "A range of values, like one to three, to leave room for bargaining and estimating."

"Okay! So we get a big skin, and we think of the little symbols we could put on it for each item, little drawing-symbols of meat or wine or cloth or a tool, and then beside it however many little round blobs for the value."

Conversation became general for several minutes until Elwin raised up his arm and said, "All right! I propose that Art and Teller figure out the details and build us a test display. Take any two of the young folks to help with the work."

And so writing was first thought of in the village.

14

The listeners gathered around the table after the evening meal. Abel asked Teller, "Friend Historian, would you just review for us your story of our beginnings? I'm hearing some different versions, and I want us to be clear about ourselves."

"Sure, I will," Teller said. "And may I ask a favor in that regard? I'd like to ask Wing to join us. He's my future replacement, you know, and I'd like to test his knowledge—and have him hear your discussion too. It'll be good schooling for him."

There was general agreement, and Teller left the group. Five minutes later (a minute was a hundred heartbeats), he returned with Wing, who nodded to his elders and silently took a seat at the table. He was a tall, slender boy of twenty summers, with brown eyes in an open, slender face and a pleasant tenor voice (he loved to sing with Ayo.)

Teller had already asked Wing to recite the opening chapter of the family history. "Are you ready?" he asked. Wing glanced around the table, looked up for about half a minute to think, then nodded.

"It was in a beautiful garden up in the mountains to the east. Our Father and Mother, Adam and Eve, awakened there. And the Maker was with them and taught them many things. Then the Maker went away, and when He returned, He was angry and sad. He said they had eaten forbidden fruit and must leave the garden and dig in the ground for their bread. They asked to be forgiven, and the Maker said, "You are made in my image. I will not abandon you."

"And they walked down the mountain."

"Was that right?" asked Wing solemnly, looking at Teller.

"Yes, that was well told, Wing." He turned to the others. "There was no more from—or about—the Maker. The story continues, of course, with how Adam and Eve lived in the forest west of the mountains, and how they had children, and families formed, and eventually separated and went their different ways."

Elwin had been silent. Now he asked, "Has the Maker abandoned us? We do not see or hear him these days. "

"I think not. He said he would not abandon us. But his time moves differently from ours. I believe he is looking after us, somehow."

"Was there anything in the story about men and women who were not sons and daughters of Adam and Eve?"

"No," answered Teller. "It wasn't denied, but it wasn't stated either. And there was a story, told later (by Adam, I suppose), about how Adam and Eve were descendants of a tribe who could not speak. That's all we know."

And they praised Wing and spoke of other things.

***

After the others had gone, Teller stayed behind. "Elwin," he said, "There's something I want to ask you."

Elwin looked up and smiled, curiosity in his eyes. "Fine. You don't ask me private questions very often. Go ahead."

Teller cleared his throat. "You've just heard again our history of Adam and Eve with the Maker, and you know how fragmentary and frustrating it is."

"That's for sure," said Elwin.

"You also know that for years I have been frustrated about having that ancient stone and thinking it has something to say about our history and having no way to listen to its story."

"Yes."

"The more I think about it, the more I believe that the stone's secret may be hidden back where our tribe originated—in Eden, where the Maker spoke to our Father and Mother. Part of the stone is missing, broken off; it may be there. They may have tried to make it speak. Other evidence might be there. It would be the journey of my life to go and see."

Elwin scratched his chin. "Do you know where Eden is? And you would have to have companions."

"From the history I know, I calculate that it must be in the mountains east of that big lake, the one we call East Lake. That's not certain. But I would hope and expect to find other humans living there who would know. And companions, yes. This journey would be a breathtaking adventure for young people who share my imagination. There are four I would like to ask: Stride, Tara, Wing, and Ayo. Stride and Tara are to be betrothed to people of the River Tribe, Priam and Binta. I would invite them also. This may all turn out to be an impossible dream, but I would like to have your permission to try."

"When would you leave? How long would it take?"

"We would leave soon after our Spring Festival with the River Tribe. It's a long journey over country we've never seen. I'd hope to arrive before the winter snows and be back about this time next year."

Elwin pondered. "You'd be taking yourself and your understudy. Without you, we'd have lost our tribal memory. But—if I were young and free, I'd give my life to go with you. You have my permission. Please return."

15

Winter camp was breaking up. They'd set off next Rest Day. Families were packing leather backpacks with flint tools, gourds, and a few bone objects such as hooks and needles. They were making new sledges—long branches fastened together with plant twine and a few cross-sticks—to hold leather tent tops and bedding shells, and some other objects necessary to a traveling group. Purndil, Artisan's handyman, was in charge of making sure these items were stowed—spear shafts, water containers, long sticks for throwing stones. And Glen was in charge of fire—its containers, its fuel, and stones to rekindle it if it were lost.

At mid-day, two young men found themselves apart from the bustle, tossing a makeshift ball around and talking about the coming party.

"We'll miss you at game time, brother," said Wing to Stride. "With Binta, you'll have other things on your mind."

"We'll still play," replied Stride, catching the ball with his left hand and scooping it back underhand between his legs. "Binta can fly through the trees. We'll be unbeatable."

"You haven't seen her since the end of summer. Wonder if she's changed?"

"I'll find out soon enough. She's to come and stay with my mother as soon as we join. Till the wedding. I'll have some new duties, I guess…."

Wing said, "Teller told me an amazing story last night. About the early times, a thousand summers ago. About language and memory and stuff. And he's got something in his bag from those times."

Wing repeated what Teller had told him.

"He thinks the markings on the stone represent what the old ones actually said. But the stone is incomplete—a piece of a larger one."

He ran back to pick up a missed throw and fired it to Stride.

"Wouldn't it be, I don't know, great, to go back and find the rest of it and figure out what it says?"

"It might, it really might," Stride mused. "But that's not where my life is headed! Hunting and babies, getting better with a spear, maybe someday telling you guys what to do."

"Don't grow old on me, buddy!" said Wing. "Let's go talk to the girls."

To Ayo and Tara, Wing repeated his talk with Teller about the mysterious stone.

Ayo thought about it and said, "Teller thinks that our family is the original one – that all the other tribes split from ours long ago. The Original Family would have kept the stone, right?"

Wing said, "He implied that, didn't he? But there's something missing. There's another part to the stone, with more symbols."

Ayo said, "How ever can we learn what it says? It looks so dramatic and full of meaning. I would love to know more about our origin and why we have … lost our way."

Wing said earnestly, "We don't know. Does another tribe have the missing piece, or – or was it left, back in the garden where everything started."

Tara said, "It's just a stone. I don't see any good in worrying about it. How could we ever find something that small in this enormous world?"

Ayo said, "If we *could* travel back to the past, to the beginning, and just watch and listen… could we understand what they were saying?"

They were all quiet for a minute, trying to imagine doing that. "How could you ever travel backward like that?" asked Wing, frowning.

"I don't know. Maybe what happens is saved somehow, and you could be taken there and shown it. What I meant was, do we speak the same language they did then?"

Then Wing stood, stamped his bare feet in the dirt a couple of times, and moved his shoulders as if preparing for a throw. He looked at the others, and they fell silent.

"Teller wants to talk to the four of us tonight. He has a proposal."

"Where?" asked Stride.

"At his tent," said Wing. "It's a good, scary proposal. I don't know the details. But be ready to be surprised."

***

After the meal and cleanup, Teller lit a small fire in his little clearing and waited beside it. The first to come was Wing, who swung down from a tree limb and landed softly just behind Teller's right shoulder. Teller listened, smiled, and said, "Joy of the evening, Wing. You arrive in style."

Wing stepped forward and squatted on his toes. He was of medium height, slim, brown-headed, with a smooth, shy face and only a sparse beard. He smiled at Teller. "They're all coming," he said.

The girls arrived together, along the ground but as silently as Wing. Tara led, small and strong, moving with an air of competence, almost impatience. But she greeted Teller respectfully and knelt at Teller's left without further conversation. Ayo greeted him, too, but went to Wing's side, kneeling on her haunches. She was his size, taller than Tara; her limbs were long, and her movements seemed adolescent, as if her growth was incomplete. Her face was serene.

All were silent for a time, listening to the night noises, automatically sorting out their causes—animal, bird, breeze. Then a little rustling of leaves and Stride appeared.

"Teller, here we are," he said. "We four have known one another—and you—since we could talk and remember. We trust you and ourselves, and we are ready for adventure. Please tell us your plan."

Teller said, "You all now know about the stone which I possess, and the symbols on it, and the secrets about our past which may be locked up in those symbols. I have been thinking about what to do with this stone and this knowledge.

"I've wondered for many years how to find out more. Sometimes, you know, I encounter other groups of men, and if a group has a historian like me, I ask them for their version of our story. None has ever seen or heard of the stone. Beyond that, their versions of our history have started to differ from mine, and over the years the differences have grown. Things are forgotten and left out or mixed up with stories and people of which our history does not speak. Slowly, we are forgetting our past.

"And lately, change has increased. Since the land has begun to warm, tribes have grown restless and divided. We meet men and are less able to speak with some of them—the words they use are changing. Their laws and traditions are changing too; I am aware of and uncomfortable with new, selfish thoughts from their leaders and a loss of our feeling of family and courtesy. And I think: if men are to discover the origin of the stone and our past, maybe it must be during my lifetime. Maybe it must be up to me. To me, and to you, my students and young friends. We need to go on a journey."

There was quiet around the fire as five pairs of eyes looked down upon the coals. Then Stride said, "What kind of journey?"

Teller stood and stretched. "Our history began, after we were swept away from the garden, with one human family. You know this; you've heard me tell the story. This family lived away to the south of the East Lake, near the mountain of the garden, growing larger, learning how to live in the world without the Maker, and wondering what to do. Stay in place or travel, split up or stay together, solve disagreements how? And it all centered around The Maker's promise that eventually He would return. Some believed it with all their hearts while others doubted. Dissensions arose, cliques formed, and eventually, families broke off and went their way. This family remained together. We became wanderers, chasing after game and food and warmth southward and westward, farther and farther from where we began. And here we are, and Earth is warming again.

He took a branch from the ground and, on a smooth, dry piece of ground, drew with it, a drawing similar to the one he'd made for Wing.

"Here is the great river, not far east of us, flowing south, they say into a great South Sea. Behind us, to the west, is another great sea around which other tribes live; we call it the Inmost Sea. And here, east and north of the great river, in high land, far and far, lies the land of our origin. I do not know how far, but surely a summer's journey.

"If memories of our fathers linger, if the missing portion of the stone exists, it must be there, in the hills whence we came. We—you young ones, strong to journey, with me as your guide, must go there and search. We must say farewell to our families, hoping to return but unsure of the future. We may fail, we may die, but we must travel now or forget the expedition forever. Elwin understands and has given his blessing. Will you come? I would like each of you to say your thoughts."

The silence stretched out as each one thought his and her own thoughts.

Wing said, "Teller, say again our goal."

"To find our history and our origin. To confirm the stories and expand them. To learn how to capture them, and much else, on stones." He raised a hand. "To find out why the Maker awoke our parents, why we are here."

More silence. Then Tara said, "I will go with you. I don't understand your vision. I'm not made that way. But I love our life together and would never leave you, my family. But—I cannot go unless Priam goes. And Stride, can you go without Binta? I say we must invite them both."

Stride nodded. "Yes, I must stay unless Binta will go with us, because I promised her, and I must keep my promise. But I love adventures, and I will happily go on this one, no matter where we travel or what we find. I think Binta will come, too."

They all looked at Ayo, and she said, "Both the world and you, my family, are precious to me. I will journey with you and make songs about everything we find, joyful or not."

Wing was last to speak. He stood up and almost danced with excitement as he spoke. "You know I love the stories. I do, but I hate that they are only fragments of the truth. I would gladly spend my life discovering more, and putting it into the stories, and marking them in stone for my own children to read. Any hardship"—he stopped and turned his head left and right—"let's do it!"

"When shall we leave?" Stride asked. And everyone spoke in a jumble of voices, calling out their agreement, asking about plans.

"Good," said Teller, turning about and almost laughing with excitement, much as Wing had done. "We must leave soon to reach our goal before winter. Here are the things we must bring with us. We leave at sunrise two days after the meeting. We will quietly ask Priam and Binta when we meet. Listen now, and get to work."

And so was created the Seven.

16

Satan sat with his lieutenants. "Belial," he said, "Report to us on our infiltrations of human tribes and villages."

"By the way, what's the difference between a tribe and a village?" Mammon interjected. "Just size?"

Satan nodded to Belial, who grinned and answered, "Yes, and it's pretty fluid. Families are related, children and maybe grandchildren. Groups of families live in villages (except for a few who choose to keep moving around), and then if the village gets big enough and important enough, has lots of families, they call it a tribe."

Belial continued, "As for us, we have two underground squadrons; Timor's, near the Eastern Lake, and Azar's, south on the River of the Tiger – that's the central one, a big squadron of builders, musicians, storytellers. They both consist of humans, ones we've recruited out of family rejects or ambitious malcontents. Loyal for the most part. We've emphasized grudges and sneers to suggest revenge. We can entice humans into the caves and hold them if they say they want to join us. They just have to say it—the Maker won't let us touch them else. And we can send them out to spread fear and keep groups from forming. Good basic tribe control." He stroked his chin. "Oh, by the way, we have contacted Cain's descendants far east of the mountains; there are several tribes and many good prospects there.

"Our active human tribes you know about: The Sun Tribe, on the eastern edge of the Inmost Sea is a large one and totally ours; they have no truck with the Maker. They worship the Sun God and are building a temple to him. The River Tribe is close, a few weak links, but most of them gone; they'll obey Sun Tribe orders. Small breakaway families have departed east and west with infiltrators, typically as assistant historians or priests (a new group we're just getting started with—you have to find a lazy leader who'll abide someone else preaching.)

"We need more large tribes like South, to inhabit the coasts and build real super-villages. Give us another three human lifetimes, and we'll have them."

"How many human villages are out there?" Satan asked.

"Maybe twenty, maybe more. I can't tell you about all the ones that have wandered off. It's a big world."

"Excellent job. Take a vacation," Satan said, laughing coarsely. "Let's all help Mammon help the Sun Tribe to finish their work. I want that temple to attract crowds of humans. Dismissed. Mammon, you stay here."

The others left, and Mammon moved closer to Satan, all attention.

Satan bent forward and rubbed his hands together. "I think it's time to invite Adam's Tribe to come deeper in. We haven't got a loyal spy in there yet, have we?"

Mammon shook his head. "No, but what we do have is this friendship between Adam and River. It goes way back; they have a big festival at the beginning of every summer. The boys at the River Tribe—Ruse and Diss—just want to take them over, like they were taken over by South.

"I'd like them to have at least a few good agents in there first. No prospects, eh? Have Slubgob tell them to keep trying. They're a high priority."

"Will do, sir."

17

The listeners were again relaxing and thinking out loud about Eden.

Elwin had been staring off into the distance. Now, he looked at them.

"It just seems to me that the Maker could not have meant for something horrible to happen to Adam and Eve right there in the garden. That part of the story bewilders me."

Teller shook his head and waved a hand. "I've thought often about that. He was teaching them how to live!"

"That's it!" muttered Elwin. "That's what I don't understand. There's got to be more to the story. How are we going to find it?"

They all stared at him, speechless.

18

The next evening, Elwin and Gratia had finished eating and were resting comfortably outside their cabin door. It was a clear, cool evening, still bright with gold in the western sky and diamonds in the dark east. As they talked, a bird fluttered down in front of them and stood quietly, peering up at them. It was forearm-long, blue-gray, with cinnamon and black on its wings.

"Well, this is a treat!" murmured Gratia. She looked the bird in the eye. "Are you hungry?"

The bird listened, then turned its head from side to side.

Gratia sat forward, now really interested. "Do you want to talk to us?"

This time, the bird nodded. "Look. Elwin, she's talking to us!"

Elwin turned and smiled. "Hello, bird. I think you're a Turtle Dove. Am I right?"

It nodded again and preened.

Elwin leaned forward, now serious. "Bird, do you come with a message for us?"

The bird nodded. "Is it a happy message?" It nodded again. "Do I know the sender?" Still another nod. "Can you tell me who it is?"

The bird stared at Elwin for a few seconds, lifted its head up, then down, and scratched the ground in a sort of circle.

"What do you suppose she means?" Elwin asked his wife.

"She means something—I'm sure of it. She turned to the bird. "May I give you a name?"

The bird nodded vigorously. "May I call you Gabriel, Gaby?" A nod and flutter of wings.

Then Elwin had an idea. "Can you show us where your sender is?

It flew upwards, eastward toward the darkness, then returned and settled.

"Can you bring us something to help us know who it is?"

Gaby thought for a minute, nodded, and flew away.

The couple looked at one another. "Well, that was fun," said Elwin.

"It was more than fun. I've got chills down my back."

"Me, too. Another mystery. Let's wait and see what it brings."

They saw the bird no more that night.

***

The next evening, when the listeners convened, Gratia told them about Gaby, the friendly and talkative bird, and about their "conversation." "It seemed really intelligent," she said. "I've never thought of an intelligent animal before."

No one had. Elwin mused, "It's not impossible. We've had reports of creatures seen in the forest, running away, maybe not humans."

Abel replied, "You're right. The idea of other creatures—besides the animals, I mean—sharing the land with us, we thought that was possible. But not a bird; more like an almost-human sort of creature who would come up and say hello."

"So it mostly nodded," said Maeve. "Could it all have been a coincidence?"

"Well, maybe," said Gratia. "But it really seemed like talking to a person. Smart but couldn't speak our language."

"It just opens up a whole new way of thinking about, oh, everything in the world. Makes it seem bigger and somehow more dangerous," said Maeve.

"I hope it comes back," said Gratia. "It may be from—oh, I don't know."

19

Down at the river, Diss had packed up and left several nights ago, with witnesses. But here he was, again at night, in Ruse's tent. He and Ruse were urging Slubgob, Satan's agent, into action.

Ruse said, "It's a major breakthrough. We have an agreement with Strut and Uruk in the South Tribe. We'll brief our tribe tomorrow; I expect only two or three who'll not join, and we can handle them. Our Spring Festival with Adam's Tribe is in two days, and we'll take them down with ease."

Slubgob shook his head. "Satan said to go slowly."

"I know," said Ruse. "But he didn't say to stop. Everything has come together. This is absolutely our opportunity, I guarantee it. And the South Tribe is chafing at the bit. They need the labor, and they mean to finish the monument by next Spring's equal day night so it can be trimmed true to dawn. It's the plan Satan wants; we'll have all the inland-sea tribes worshipping the sun!"

Diss chimed in: "Elwin's people were completely fooled. But you know, we can't keep it secret forever; someone will talk. Satan will be so pleased!"

Ruse rubbed his hands together. "This is fine!"

Slubgob sat silent, head down. Finally, he looked up. "All right. We'll brief Satan as soon as you succeed. Don't fail."

20

Adam's Family met with the River Tribe on an open plain that swept down to the Great River southwestward. This plain was a long day's march north of their village, where the river had broad, swooping curves. North and east were dense forest with a tributary stream joining the river from the east. On the west, the plain opened across the river and through the woods, creating a broad lane for the setting sun's gold from a sky with dark clouds building.

The River Tribe made its camp on the river's east bank, up which they had journeyed. From there, the men strode into the plain to meet with their counterparts. A great fire was built, food was brought out and cooked, and precious stores of fermented juice appeared. The talk was steady and occasionally boisterous.

Teller walked around the periphery of the fire in the dusk, looking for Wing. But the youths were gone. They'd all been there an hour ago when the betrothal of two couples had been celebrated: Stride from Adam's Family with Binta from the River Family and Tara from Adam's Family to Priam from River. In each case, the women would leave their Tribes and join the men who would become their husbands. The weddings would take place after the summer travels.

There were sports: stone throwing, at which Stride was supreme; running races, with Tara sprinting to the lead of the women; and the tree game, where teams threw a large ball (leather stuffed with leaves) around a circle and up to a teammate in a tree to try jamming it through a circular branch-net set on a limb. Sometimes, someone fell out of the tree, but no harm was done.

Later, the Seven's youths withdrew to the eastern end of the camp to prepare and pack for the journey.

Teller walked and worried. Should he share their plans with South's leaders? Two of their young, Binta and Priam, would be taking part. The journey was to be long and dangerous, a virtual step into the unknown; nothing like it had ever been attempted. But somehow, these facts made him reluctant to share them with leaders he didn't quite trust, men who whispered secretly among themselves. What if they tried to stop the journey, refused to allow their young ones to go?

He didn't know them well enough. Better to wait.

There was a shout over by the fire, then another, then silence. That wasn't right. Teller stopped and moved a little closer to see. What was happening?

The fire was brighter now in the last red glow of sunset. Elwin stood close to it with Gratia and Stride's mother and her female companion. He was talking with Ruse, the leader of River Family. In the group were Ruse's new assistant Laeso, Elwin's deputy Stane, and two men from River whom Elwin didn't know. Nearby, the men of both tribes mingled and drank together, with most of the women in separate groups. River Tribe men casually moved closer to Adam's people.

Elwin said, "You have prospered, Ruse. There are more here this Spring than at our last."

"Yes, we are many now." Ruse smiled and looked behind and around him. He raised his right arm, and the gesture was repeated by River men around them. Ruse said, "I will now suggest a change of plans for our respective Summer travels." Then he turned and shouted, "Take them now!"

Elwin and his men were unarmed and unwarned. Elwin shouted, "Family to arms!" But Ruse had a club tipped with a sharp stone. He swung it at Elwin's head. Elwin ducked, but the blow left him down. Ruse struck again, at Stane, killing him with the blow. Laeso grabbed Gratia's companion around her neck from behind and broke it with a violent twist. Another River man knocked Gratia to the ground and bound her arms with hemp. Through the group, armed River Family men attacked unarmed Adam's Family men and women, captured them if possible, or killed them. It was over in minutes.

Ruse shouted, "Prisoners to our camp, guard them! Guards, follow me to their camp; we'll take the rest!

Teller had been watching in stunned silence; he turned and disappeared at a run into the forest, to where his young teammates were gathered.

"Everyone! Everyone!" he shouted. Then he paused for a moment, squeezed his eyes shut, thought, and opened them. He spoke in an intense but quiet voice.

"The River men have attacked us. They are killing or capturing everyone. Stane is dead." He shook his head. "We must leave NOW, on the run. Get the supplies you have prepared and follow me eastward. If it's not close by, leave it. Now, now! Two minutes to gather; we will go to the tree and wait that long."

There was a brief noise as the six youths gasped. Then all disappeared except Wing and Stride, who, without a word, followed Teller eastward into the dark forest, moving fast and as silently as possible.

The tree was in a clearing, four minutes away, where the young ones played their games. The three crouched silently at its eastern edge, behind the tallest tree. Very soon, others came, lightly, listening for whispers, looking for moving shadows as their eyes adjusted to the starry night and joined. Priam and Tara, then Ayo.

"Where's Binta?" whispered Teller.

Ayo whispered, "Oh, she was looking for a cloak for Stride."

Stride: "I can't go without her."

They waited. They heard noises in the brush, distant but coming nearer, and men's voices, cursing and shouting. "This way! Here's his fire. Damn that old man."

Stride whispered, soft but hissing with intensity. "Three of them at most. Up in the trees, carry your stones, now!"

Teller: "Go! I'll draw them here."

Teller crept silently back toward the fire. Close enough to see, he crouched immobile except for his eyes, which darted left and right, counting and evaluating the enemy. There were three men. The leader was tall and looked strong and quick; he carried a stick with a sharp object embedded in its tip. The other two were smaller and younger, armed the same way.

"They were here minutes ago," said one.

"And here are footprints and a broken branch," said the other. "Look, they left in two directions. Over here, too. Most of them went this way."

The leader hissed, "Go down that way. Never mind noise. Shout, it makes them afraid. Kill them." He turned and went alone up the first way.

Teller had been about to make a noise to draw them after him, but now he was silent and still. This was very good. They'd split up! He let the leader tread quietly up the path and followed not too close behind. It was dark, but he found a rock and carried it.

The five in the trees had rocks, too. They watched with silent intensity as the two young men, armed, trotted into the clearing, stopped, and peered around. Their shapes were grayly visible to those above. Stride waited. When the two remained stationary, he hissed again. "Throw."

Their game was now a deadly battle. Five rocks flew out of the branches toward the men. One dropped, and the other shouted and jumped sideways. "Down!" shouted Stride and leaped from his branch, falling like a rock, feet first, on the second man's back. In seconds, both enemies were dead or unconscious.

The leader was making his way back to the youths' gathering place, silently followed by Teller. Embers of a fire were still alight, and in their light, the leader saw a shadowy figure beyond, crouched, pulling things up and tossing them aside. He stood tall, ready to shout and attack, but Teller shouted first. "Binta down!"

Binta ducked and rolled. The enemy leader threw his stone, missed, and leaped. Teller's stone did not miss. He made sure the leader would not breathe again.

"Come." He led in the direction of the tree, and Binta followed.

"It is I," whispered Teller as he and Binta entered the clearing. The others gathered quickly and closely; all seven were here. Stride briefly touched Binta. They listened intently for one minute, and then Teller spoke.

"We will start our journey now. On this night, we are not traveling; we are escaping. The most important things are speed, keeping together, and protecting one another. No scouts, single file." Briefly, they agreed on hand signals and voice signals that would blend with forest sounds.

"Now for the route. The river is west of us, but it sweeps north and eastward. We should go eastward for an hour, then turn to the north and cross it for safety. Stride, do you remember the ford?"

"Yes."

"Then lead us. Next Wing, then Tara, Ayo, Priam, Binta. I will be last. Stay together! Speed is more important than silence now."

A branch rustled, and a small, thin figure appeared. "It's me, Aaron," he whispered. "I can't go back. Can I come with you?"

Teller made an instant decision. He said, "Yes! Stay by my side!"

Stride walked to the east side of the clearing, stopped for a deep breath, looked behind him for Wing, a shadow in the darkness, and set off. His pace was not a run, but his stride was long and graceful.

21

Now, the dark was deeper, and the forest and its animal paths were strange. The seven, now eight, were crossing an open area; there were more of these between woods. Above them, the constellations had wheeled westward, and a faint gleam on the horizon ahead presaged the rising of the late old moon. Their walking pace was fast and dogged.

Atop a rise, Stride stopped and signaled silently for the rest to close up. Together, they stood and listened. The land was never without sound. There was a quiet background of the wind through nearby brush and distant trees. There were odd scuffling sounds of animals making their way, hidden even in the dark. No bird sounds and no sounds of human movement.

Stride turned to his right and spoke. "The river is that way, north, a hundred minutes, I think. Best we move ahead into the valley, drink at the little stream, then turn and follow it. We can ford the river there—it isn't too deep—and move northeast along its banks. What do you think, Teller?"

"An hour's journey. Perhaps three hours until sunup, enough time to put more distance behind us, then settle in for rest. Is everyone all right? Any injuries?"

There were none. Wing said, "I'm thirsty, and so are you, I think. There'll be water at the stream. We need not eat until we rest."

Tara said, "We need to reassign burdens now, even them out, leave the fighters more free in case we fight. Then soon, we'll need to stop, camp, find food and clothing, and prepare for the long walk. Teller, how many more suns must we run?"

Teller said, "Perhaps three suns without being followed."

An hour is a hundred minutes, each sun (day) ten hours, a moon four times seven suns, a year or Summer thirteen moons.

He turned around among the travelers, touching them on the shoulder one by one, judging their courage, fatigue, and confusion.

"Let's follow Stride's plan. We'll stop at the stream, drink, and redistribute our loads."

Ayo whispered, "Let's join hands for just a moment." They did and were silent until Binta said, "Maker, give us strength and understanding."

Then Stride turned and raised his right arm, and they fell into their line.

The seven moved, as silently as they could, northward along the stream toward the river. The old moon was above the eastern horizon, softening the darkness a little and making it more dangerous. A gentle north wind was blowing. They had drunk, rested briefly, and redistributed burdens. Stride now shared the lead with Teller and Priam; Wing went last, alert for followers. The women were more heavily burdened, but they were strong and fit and bore their loads lightly.

They stopped and listened in silence. Below the trickle of their stream, the lower rumble of deeper, slower water could now be heard. A few night sounds—nothing out of place—but Teller was not satisfied. He listened longer, turned right and left, raised his head, and sniffed the air, slowly and deeply.

"Humans." He whispered. "Which side of the river are they on?"

Stride listened for a minute, then shook his head.

"Closer," he mouthed.

Teller nodded and extended his arms in a "spread out" gesture. The others nodded; Stride moved left and Priam right, and they moved forward in silence, keeping abreast by the merest traces of sight and sound.

As the sound of the river grew louder, the leaders came to the edge of the trees into an open space. Teller waited till the others drew closer, then gestured them to stay hidden. Crouching, the three crept forward to the top of an incline. They could see the river in the moonlight a hundred yards away.

They waited again, straining every sense. A minute. Two. Three. Then Stride raised his hand and beckoned the other two to him.

He pointed left and down. The dark shape of a man stood bent, his back to them, his feet in the water. A smaller, dark shape was at his right hand.

More waiting, no other signs of men or animals. Teller whispered, "We can wait, but sunup will bring greater risk. We can go right and ford the river quietly. Or we can accost this person. I think fording is the best course."

Each young man nodded his "yes," and they crouch-walked back to the women and Wing. Teller was glad that neither boy had a lust for fighting now. They are grown for their years, he thought. They moved back into the trees and whispered a conference.

"He might be a friend," said Tara.

"Indeed he might," Teller responded. "But I will feel safer if no one at all sees us now until we are far away from the massacre."

Ayo asked, "What is that with him?"

Teller said, "I don't know. But I have heard of animals who follow men."

Stride said, "Let's move east for half an hour, then cross to the north side." And they started moving to their right, keeping under the trees, stopping periodically to listen.

Judging by guess and by the stars, Stride stopped. All listened intently for a minute, and then Stride led them carefully down toward the water. Arriving, they watched, listened, and finally drank. Then they spread out, looking for the best place to ford. The river was fairly broad and quiet here, with shallows; it reflected the moonlight when clouds permitted. Wing found a spot off to the right, and they slowly entered the water in single file, carrying their weapons or packs at shoulder height. The current was strong but steady, and the bottom was firm sand. Soon, they were nearly across.

A shadow moved to their left, and a voice said, in a conversational tone, "So here you are. I've been wanting a chat."

Everyone froze. Then Stride and Priam pushed their way to the stranger's right and left while Teller faced him.

The man was of medium height and appeared slender (though it was hard to tell in the darkness.) His hands were empty.

Teller said, "Was that you at the ford?"

The stranger replied, "Yes, that was I. My friend Dog is on the north bank waiting for me. I suggest we proceed there and get acquainted on dry land."

He turned to his left to face the north shore about twenty feet away, then waited for the group's reaction.

Teller looked around at his people, nodded, and said, "Let's go." He led the group toward the shore with the stranger at his side.

Teller found a dry, grassy spot and sat, and the others sat around him in the moonlight. He said to the stranger, "Tell us about yourself. Why have you followed us?"

"I am called Walker by those I have met in my travels. The name my parents gave me was Striver; they were curious people who sought new knowledge and hoped that I would seek it, too, when I was grown. I have lived seventy summers.

"We were part of a family that settled on the southeast shore of the Inmost Sea six lifetimes ago. For a long time, this family lived in peace, hunting and gathering food on land and fish in the sea. We learned how to build and manage rafts and push them about a little near the shore—and we were good swimmers." He chuckled at a private memory.

"But when I was a young man—the age of your companions, more or less—our quiet life was changed. A family, larger than ourselves, came out of the south and occupied land near us. They were friendly but secretive and mostly kept to themselves. And they carried out rituals—killing small animals and birds, daubing the blood on themselves, chanting in words we did not recognize, different from the common language of men.

"Our family did not wish to take part. We have our own stories of the past. But my parents were curious, asked to observe, and were granted it occasionally. They told me that these people seemed impatient with our stories, wanted more, and were seekers, too. But I did not like the young ones I met; they had their own clique and treated me like a nuisance, not a friend.

"I'll make a long story short. Within two summers, ill will had developed between the groups to the point of angry confrontation. It finished with my family being threatened and forced northward. And I went off on my own and have been on my own ever since."

Walker fell silent and cleared his throat, eyes on Teller.

Teller said, "That was half a lifetime ago. You must have interesting stories to tell. Tell us what sort of life you have led, what adventures you have had."

Walker smiled. "My whole story would take days, and you do not even have until sunup to spare. But I will tell you a little now and more in the future if we meet again.

"Once I was alone and safe, I devoted my time to learning better how to live, eat, and travel safely; that included a little self-defense. Then I moved around this world of ours, north and east in the summer, south and west in winter—you know how cold the winters were years ago. I studied the plan of it and have drawn it on bark. I studied the animals and have made a friendship with one of them. I encountered, in this long time, seven different groups of humans and one not-quite-human group. I've tried to learn from all of them—language, history, nature, belief—while not joining with any of them. I think my parents would be proud of me."

Stride broke in. "Do you know the River Family? And do you know why we are running eastward?"

All eyes fastened on Walker with a mixture of mistrust and fascination.

Walker said, "Yes. At least I know part of the story. The River Tribe has become subservient to the family I fled from in my youth, which has strayed far from our vision of the world and of our past. They dwell on the eastern shore of the Inmost Sea and east of your village, down there" —he gestured to the southwest. "They call themselves the Sun Family. They have big ideas and much self-importance. They commanded the River Tribe to ambush you because they need slaves for their big ideas, to carry them out."

Teller stood and said, "Walker, I am tempted to trust you, but I have no reason to. If we simply part, why will you not report us to Ruse and bring him after us?"

Walker said, "I understand you. I am a stranger, and I know things about you that I might have learned from your enemy. But if I were in league with them (which the Maker forbid), would I not have simply spied and reported secretly?"

Teller thought. "Do you know of our mission? Not who we are escaping, but what we are seeking?"

"That I do not."

"Then let it remain with us for now. We could perhaps benefit greatly from your knowledge, but I am not ready to ask it yet."

Walker nodded. "Let us part friends and see what the future brings." He arose, and the dog came closer to him. "Go northeast, away from the river. There is danger to the south."

He turned and glided away into the trees.

Teller said, “Let us be on our way now and make as much distance as we can. After that and sleep, we’ll talk again.”

22

Those still alive of Elwin's stricken family were hurried along in the darkness by suddenly fearsome strangers. Their hands were tied behind them by ropes made of twisted vines. A vine noose was put around each person's neck, the other end in the hand of a River Family man turned soldier. The soldiers had sticks and did not hesitate to use them to keep their prisoners on pace.

Stane and four other men were dead. Gratia's aide, Ahura, was dead too. Others were injured, and in the darkness and confusion, two children were missing. But that was of no concern to their captors. On they moved in the moonlight along a river path southward, stumbling and falling and getting up. There was no attempt at silence.

***

Elwin's head hurt, but he was able to walk—and to think. In the dark, he recognized Artisan's voice ahead of him by his grunts and occasional oaths. Stane had been Elwin's second-in-command. He knew Stane was dead, and he knew his people would desperately need a leader now. He would have to make contact. Who was left to be his deputy, and how could he do it? Dark thoughts festered in his mind as he stumbled along the path.

After endless hours of pain and numbness, the east lightened, and the column halted. The prisoners were allowed to relieve themselves and sit, still tied and guarded. Elwin counted about fifty of them, all adults except for two teenagers and two younger children, each pair a boy and a girl. They were brought water to drink and a few roots to chew.

Elwin had managed to come close to Artisan. "Friend, how are you?" he asked in a soft voice, almost a whisper. "Alive," was the reply.

"You and I have to hold the family together," Elwin said.

"If we can. Where are we? Can you tell?"

"Still near the river, moving south. Ten miles from camp, I think. Let's talk to the others for a moment." He looked around silently, then reached out and took the hand of the nearest.

"Gratia," he whispered. "We're here. Take hands all," in a louder whisper. Faces peered at him, and recognition came over them. Slowly, hands were clasped until almost all were connected.

Gratia whispered to him, "You were nearly killed. Are you all right?"

"Yes."

She said, "You are still our leader."

Elwin whispered, "Yes. Guide the women if we are separated." Then to all, "Pray."

And he began, 'Maker, be with us, Maker, help us, keep us from harm.'"

The prayer was repeated again and again.

"Be quiet!" said a guard loudly and struck Elwin on the face with his stick.

"Be consoled," Elwin said and was silent. His two goals had been achieved: the family was a unit again, and its captors knew who was their leader.

***

It was a clear, hot morning, and the male prisoners were being herded to the Temple for work. Winnie watched them and noted their loss of weight, tattered fragments of clothing, and grim, expressionless faces. Art glanced over, noticed her watching, and gave her a brief smile.

She stayed with the other women, watched by one of the guards. "Gratia," she murmured, "have you watched that guard before? He seems to me more patient with us. And he looks tired this morning."

Gratia nodded. "I watch them all. This one I'm not afraid of. He seems human."

Winnie said, "I have an idea. I'm going to talk to him."

She sidled over near the guard. "Guard," she said. "I am the one who gathers medicine for these people. I know about herbs and seeds that can help with sickness."

"Oh?" said the guard.

"I think there may be good herbs in these fields. Will you let me look?"

The guard frowned at her. "What kind of troubles?

"Pain, headache, stomachache, sore backs, bleeding."

He looked at her more closely. "Who are you?"

"Winnie. Elwin is my leader."

"Can you make my head stop hurting?"

"I might. Will you let me look?"

"Oh, all right. Go that way." He pointed north toward the stream. "Stay in sight."

She bowed and said, "In case another guard challenges me, what's your name?"

"Ham."

"I'll see what I can find."

Winnie turned and began to walk slowly away, her head down, looking at the ground.

She did not return for several hours. When she did, she sought out Ham. "Sir, take these leaves and chew them slowly.

They'll taste bitter; your mouth will get a little numb. They'll help your head."

He took the leaves, and she returned to the group, holding her other finds under her robe.

23

In the afternoon sunshine, Tara and the others were making camp.

They had made their way as quickly as possible in the darkness parallel to the river, their aim pointing north of the rising moon and then of the sun. They broke out of forest cover into a meadow, uphill but easier going. Finally, on an east-west ridge, in trees again, they felt safe enough to stop for rest, thirty miles from the slaughter-bloodied camp and ten miles clear of the river. (A mile is a thousand steps, the distance at which a large animal can be spotted.)

The sun was warm on their shoulders, and the meadow around them was a burst of color—blue and orange and yellow and white, with flowers of every size and kind.

A place was selected that was flat enough for cooking and sleeping and had approaches that could be watched. There was no water there, but a stream had been crossed less than a mile ago, and all had drunk their fill, washed and filled the three bowls that would serve for cooking. Teller rested. The other men and Binta were foraging. Tara and Ayo prepared a space for the fire and brought kindling to it, and some small leafy branches for beds. The last forty hours had left them too tired to think coherently.

"Well, we're off on our great adventure," Tara muttered as she arranged kindling and stones.

Ayo spread animal-hide cloaks over the bedding branches. "It's terrible."

"We're all the family we've got now."

Two of the bowls were of hollowed-out wood. The largest was of clay. It had been formed years ago and so carefully baked and annealed closer and closer to the cooking fires that now it was strong and could sit above a fire on thick wooden Y-shaped sticks, protected by its own charred surfaces, as long as it had water in it.

Stride and Priam were foraging together among the trees. Stride glanced sideways at Priam and said, "We were gathering our possessions for this trip before the attack. You weren't. What do you need?"

Priam was kneeling, trying to dig up a potato-like root with his fingers. "I could use a bone knife if you have another one."

"Wait," said Stride, and he lowered his sack to the ground and burrowed in it. "Here, try this one." He held out the foreleg bone of a deer, sharpened at one end.

"Thanks," said Priam. He dug some more. "Well, we're alive and not captured, we can say that much. But do you think we should just be running away like this?"

Stride stopped to think. He said, "I haven't thought it out yet. We sure can't fight your whole family, just the seven of us." He found a leaf, put it in his mouth and chewed, swallowed it, and put several more in his sack.

Then he continued, "Where can we find help? Maybe that family that lives west of us. I don't know. Teller will talk to us once we're safely away."

Priam grunted. "Is this search of yours so important? Will we find help this way?"

"We might, you know." Stride turned to look at Priam. "It's an important search, it really is."

The foragers returned, carrying their leaves and roots and one large rabbit, killed with a stone. Wing was the best fire-starter; he coaxed a flame with the two stones that sparked when rubbed together—precious, irreplaceable tools. Ayo added vegetables and a powder to the heating water while Stride stripped the animal of skin and guts, using sharp flints to cut it into pieces. These were browned briefly in the fire and then went into the pot.

They shared food and water, and Teller talked. He spoke of old legendary travels through the twenty-generation, thousand-summer history of the family, of storms and scary nights, how one learned how to create and carry fire, how fine it was to have children around to play with, of catching fish and singing together.

"And tomorrow, after a good sleep, we'll talk about where we are and where we're going." Then, thoughtfully, "There are different kinds of evil. We and our fathers faced the first kind, this indifferent world that goes its own way, nurturing or destroying us. The second is the evil that seems to grow within us. And the third... well, enough of that for tonight. We are not merely threatened. We are looked after, too."

They smothered the fire, set the guard, and slept. In the distance, Walker watched their camp.

***

Morning dawned clear and cool. There had been sounds of snuffling and scurrying, but no dangerous animals or humans threatened them. The birds around and above them sang and chatted like a collection of friendly strangers.

The eight awoke, relieved themselves away from the camp, and gathered plants and water, mostly in silence. Then, they sat in their circle to eat. Already, a grouping had arisen: on Teller's right sat Stride, then Binta, then Priam; on his left sat Wing, Ayo, then Tara. Tara was next to Priam in the circle.

"Teller," Tara said. "This adventure doesn't feel as I thought it would. There's been death; we are fleeing. It's not an adventure. Does our goal mean anything now?"

Teller said, "Let's talk about that now." He looked around at each face. Tara was grim, almost defiant. Stride was calm. Priam was glum, looking at the ground. The others were staring at Teller.

"We looked at this quest as the adventure of our lives," he said, "walking into the unknown, looking for truth in the beginnings of our race. We hoped we would return older, wiser, healthy, full of our story, and with evidence that we humans could begin to keep a record of what we thought, did, and believed. We dreamed that we might become known afar as the first recorders." He smiled. "At least, I did.

"Now we are fleeing. People we loved are dead. Others are probably slaves, bound for what fate we do not know. We may have no families to return to. We may be all that's left of our family now, doomed to start over in sorrow and a sense of failure, worse off than before.

"But our quest is still before us. It is as important as it was, as challenging as anything that will ever come into our lives. Let's continue. And let's pledge that after our search is over we will return to find our lost people, recruit allies, and somehow free them."

Tara had listened restlessly. She said, "Teller, I am too sad and angry to share your hope. But, but—I trust you, and you are my leader now." She looked around at the faces. "And I love you all. You are my family. Whatever we do, let's do it together."

Then Binta spoke. "I am even more anguished and uncertain than you, Tara. My family gave me to yours to be married into you…." She glanced at Stride, who looked back with steady kindness, "and then they committed this terrible thing—and would have killed or enslaved us too. I feel such guilt. Who is my family? Who is my family?"

Stride said, "I am your family, Binta."

Teller said, “We are your family and Priam’s too.” He looked at Priam, who nodded but did not speak. “What are your thoughts, young warrior?”

Priam cleared his throat. “I share Binta’s horror at what my family’s leaders have done. My parents, my teachers, would never have done this. They are victims too… Should we could go back now and help them?”

Teller nodded. “That’s the right question, Priam. Where does duty lie? There is a family west of our winter grounds that we have known a little. We hear of another south and west on the shores of the Inmost Sea. We don’t know them. There’s a chance we could double back around our enemies—we don’t know where they’re going, but I suspect back down the River—and find another family and ask to join them. They might allow that. I think none would ally themselves with us, strangers, to do battle and rescue our own. So this would just be another way to start life over again. I think our best hope for allies lies ahead.” He stopped now and looked around, while the others thought.

Finally, Wing spoke. “Trust and hope are stronger in me with my family than with any strangers. We may never find the garden at all. But if we do, we may find allies there and still remain a family. I want to go on.”

“Are there other thoughts?”

No one answered. Teller said, “I agree with Wing. Priam, will you place your future with us?”

Priam said, “Yes.”

At this, young Aaron, who had been silently keeping to Teller’s side, lifted up his head. “Thank you for saving me. I don’t look strong, but I am. I’ll keep up with you and find food and carry my share of the load.”

Teller put his hand on Aaron’s shoulder. “Of course, you will. Shall we continue then?”

One by one, the young men and women nodded.

"Good. Let us plan our journey as best we can. And there is one more piece of advice that I must give you now. You are young and vigorous. You are thrown together by common danger into a most intimate group. The temptation to couple will be great. But you should avoid it. Our journey is not a summer picnic; it's a campaign. Nature, weather, animals, and men will be against us. Cold, poverty, and starvation will threaten us. Having one of us with child, and later an infant to care for, could cause us to fail. Let us, for the sake of our comradeship, wait until our quest is ended to marry, couple, and raise our children."

That was silently taken in by the six: Priam and Tara, who were betrothed; Stride and Binta, who were expected to be; Ayo and Wing, single but drawn together.

Teller said, "Stride, Binta, let us plan today's trek."

24

Teller had said their journey was not just a summer treat. But high summer was coming, and the country was kind to the travelers. If they had possessed writing, a log of their journey might have read thus:

"Day One: sufficient food on hand, pressed for distance. The River has turned northeast and appears again on our right. Stayed north of it and walked northeastward along a broad plain covered in grasses and trees lining brooks and streams. High land can be seen northward in haze, far away. Southward, the land trends down gently, and forest can be seen in the distance. Mid-day pause at brook, ate vegetables collected as we walked and a little dried meat. At sunset, a travel camp, dry, no fire, food same as mid-day, water from stores. Slept undisturbed.

"Day Two: still on march. Explored a valley running northeast, containing a tributary stream, flowing southward opposite our direction. Found fruits and roots for food stores. Small animals are seldom seen in the plain, but where there are trees, there are animals in them and in the brush. Near the valley's stream, found droppings and other signs of larger animals. Travel camp.

"Day Three: valley is turning north. Made camp in the bend, sent teams out to forage. Stride's team killed a hoofed short-haired animal, called it a 'goat' and dressed it out for food, skin, and bone. Tara and Binta fished with nets and caught several small flatfish. We had a fire and cooked the fish for mid-day, saving the meat for the sunset meal. No signs of human or animal approach. All slept peacefully.

"Day Four: Sunshine and full bellies have made the team happier and more active; good conversation as we breakfasted and broke up camp. Left the valley by climbing the ridge on our right to get back on our northeastward course. We want to stay between the river and the northern mountains until we have to climb, and that is weeks ahead. Foraging as we walk. Travel camp."

***

In this manner, the eight made their easting in a relaxed lope, stopping every third or fourth day when food or water needed replenishing. For many days, they were not troubled with need or threat and lived in the present, putting the future away from their thoughts.

Then Walker was spotted again.

It was in the evening, at the end of a foraging day, in a copse containing a spring-fed pond. They had a small fire, but Stride had set lookouts, and Wing spotted him, far across the plain to the south, walking openly with his dog. He saw Wing and waved his arm.

Among the group, Walker sat and accepted water and a piece of meat. He ate and drank quickly, wiped his hands on leaves, and said, "I bring you news of your families. May I speak?" Teller looked around at the faces, all tense with interest, and nodded.

"Seven days ago and far to the south, I encountered a young man whom I knew from years ago. His family lived near the Inmost Sea, near the place I grew up in.

"Two summers ago, another family appeared. They were known to this man's family, which I shall call the Inland-Sea

Family, and had followed them north along the shore of the Sea. These people were different. They had wood and stone tools which had not been seen before. They carried sacks of things, things besides food and medicine—ornaments, carvings, bright tiny stones and glass, which the women and the men wore.

"They had no Teller. They said that the old stories were oppressive and not true and that they had found gods and truth in the sea. They worshipped these gods and had come north to make some monument to them so that wealth and power would be theirs, unlike the poor tribes who clung to stories about the garden. And one morning, they attacked the Inland-Sea Family, killed their leaders, and made slaves of the rest.

"They called themselves the 'Sun' Family.

"They herded their prisoners eastward to the Great River, where other slaves were being held. Then they sent men east of the river to a place in the hills where stone outcroppings were. With the labor of their slaves, they are dragging stones together to make something to worship. And this man saw, not three weeks ago, men and women of your family brought from the northwest to be slaves too. He managed to speak to one or two of them. Then he managed to run away. I found him hiding, miles north of where all this is taking place."

The group sat staring down, stunned.

Teller said, "What was this man's name?"

Walker replied, "His name is Kelso. He is a young man."

"Did he tell you the names of any of our people? How many were there?"

"He overheard one being called 'Elwin.' No more. He guessed about forty of them were there."

Teller said, "Elwin. Our leader. He is a good, strong man. He will help the others to survive."

Priam had been looking from one to the other, his mouth open. "Who—did he name any of those other slaves?"

Walker thought and answered, "No. The great Sun family men stayed aloof from the prisoners, except for providing guards and directing the monument building. River Family people assisted them. He knew several of them. The only name he mentioned was Ruse, one of its leaders."

Priam looked up, looking unfocused, then bent and put his face in his hands.

"There has to be a reason," cried Binta, shaking her head. She went to Priam and put her hands on his shoulders.

Teller said, "Walker, what you have told us has put us in great confusion. We will have to think and discuss this news and decide what to do if it is true. Can you tell us anything else?

Walker considered. "All this is happening several days journey to the south. Kelso is hiding down there; I told him that I had friends to the north and would tell them his story. He needs help and friendship. The builders have many men armed with spears. Alone, you can do nothing to help your friends."

"What about others escaping from the builders, tribesmen of Kelso?" Stride asked.

"No one so far."

"All right," said Teller. "Will you camp away from us so that we may counsel and sleep over your news? Then return in the morning. Please?"

"I will," said Walker. He and the dog trudged off down the hill.

***

Teller sat back down and looked at his friends one by one.

"This is sad and startling. Our family in slavery to the south and Priam and Binta's family giving aid to their captors. We need to see whether we can agree on what to do. I'd like to hear from each of you, from the heart, with no one taking offense. Priam and Binta, I will call on you last. Stride?"

Stride looked around at each person's eyes, much as Teller had done.

"I am thinking as I speak," he said. "I thought my family was dead. Knowing where they are makes it harder. It makes us think that we can go and rescue them."

He paused, looking at the ground, and shook his head. "We can't. We're not strong enough. I think we have to keep going, going eastward. But we have to find help. Our mission has changed."

Teller nodded at Tara. She looked at Binta and said, "I want to go to help your family. And I think our family will be your family too—Priam and I—after what's happened. But I agree with Stride that we cannot go now. We must seek allies on our journey and become strong enough to rescue them on our return."

Then, it was Ayo's turn. "Like Tara, I will do anything to save our family if we can. May you find the way for us to bring it about."

Teller said, "Wing, what are your thoughts?"

Wing had listened and watched with intense attention, observing the language of his companions' eyes and bodies as well as their words. He stood up and faced the circle.

"Since I was a little boy, I have listened to Teller's stories and memorized them. Our story, the story of the men and women who made our family, is more important than life to me, and this journey is the greatest opportunity of my life. But what we want isn't always what we can have. We have to eat and sleep and stand between our family and evil. So—I want to do both, and right now I don't know how. Maybe," he turned to Teller, "maybe we should ask that this Kelso come up north and join us on our way and tell us everything he has seen."

Tara said, "But we don't know him—"

Teller cut her off. "Before we discuss, let's hear from Priam and Binta."

The pair of young people from the River Family looked at one another. Priam looked at Binta, and Binta spoke.

"Tara said that I and Priam were now of your family, not the one we grew up with. I love her for saying that, and I agree. The River Family are no longer my family; you are. So I will agree to your plans and help you in all ways." She looked at Priam again, and now Priam rose to his feet.

He said, "This is impossible. My heart has been torn by pain and confusion since that night of massacre and flight. I loved my family and agreed to leave them to go with you, thinking that our two tribes would always be friends, growing and ruling in the forests and by the sea." He stared away as if seeing something in the southern sky.

"But that is not going to happen. I will stay with you. I don't want to raise my hand against my father and my mother. But—here I am." He sat down and stared at nothing.

Teller said, "Thank you all for speaking your minds. Let's sleep now, and in the morning, I will tell you my plan for your approval before we meet again with Walker."

25

In daylight, the eight broke their fast, and Teller spoke to them as they ate. The mood was quiet and tense.

"I thought long about your statements last night, and it came to me how selfish and thoughtless I was to entice you into this trip in the first place. I've had my whole lifetime to roll our history around in my head, to wonder exactly how our story started, what was said, and what happened. I have longed to find someone to talk to who might know more than I do or some record left behind of what seems to have been a reaching into our world from its maker. Having the fragment made it all seem feasible. I just could not resist the opportunity to enlist your youth and strength in my odyssey.

"But this morning, I realize the audacity and am crushed by it. We are so few. Such a fragment of scattered humanity. Such a dangerous country, with storms and cliffs and wild animals. And now, worst of all, of humans whose minds are filled with dark visions and selfish dreams, who wish us dead."

He paused. Stride looked up from his food and said, "Teller, remember that it was you who saved us, swept us up, and escaped with us from death or captivity. We're lucky to be where we are, to have a chance to help our families. We can do it."

Teller smiled. "Yes, we can. We are few, with few weapons and no magic. But the dangers make the prize all the greater to me. And I agree with your majority opinion. And I agree with Stride. Saving our family is now our greatest mission, if not our first.

"I am going on. I pray that all of you will join me."

In a jumble of words, all six said, "Yes, I will" or "Count me in."

"Then," said Teller, "let us think about some things. First, I agree that we should ask that Kelso be invited to come north to intercept us. It is our duty to find out all he knows, and if he is a good man, he will increase our strength. This is a risk—both Walker and now Kelso know more about us than I thought safe; our safety in hiding has been compromised. But it would have happened eventually. Let's bid him come."

Priam asked, "What family is he from?"

Teller said, "I interpret Walker to have said that he was not from your family or ours (obviously), nor from the family to which your family is bringing captives. He seems to be from a fourth family, one that lived on the shore of the Inmost Sea northwest of the Great River. In fact, he may be from the family Walker came from."

Priam replied, "So now we are dealing with four separate Tribes. How many are there in the world?

Teller shrugged, "No one knows. It's been nearly twenty lifetimes since the beginning. The family first split up about a hundred years after the beginning. There could be dozens now. The Earth seems endless, spreading out in all directions, mountains and seas. What lands lie beyond the seas? We know nothing of that. Shall Kelso join us?"

Again, there was a murmur of assent.

"And shall we trust Walker with knowledge of our mission? Do we trust him enough?"

"Our mission to reach the mountains?" asked Priam.

Teller said, "Forgive my fussy precision. Our mission is not to reach the mountains. Our first mission was to find the origin of my stone and how language may be captured. To accomplish, that we'll reach and search the mountains. Our second mission is to rescue our families. Shall we tell Walker about all of it?"

Stride said, "I don't see why we should keep it from him now."

The others nodded their agreement.

"All right, then," said Teller, "—oh, wait, I see Walker coming up to meet with us."

Walker joined them and accepted food and water. His dog accepted some scraps, then took himself to the top of the slope and sat, quiet and alert.

"What have you decided?" Walker asked.

Teller said, "We have decided to ask you to send Kelso to us. But we'd like to know more about him. Tell us what you know, please."

Walker sat chin in hand for a moment. "As I told you, he is a young man from an Inmost Sea family. I do not know his parents, but I knew his family and respected its leaders. And he had the courage to approach me after his escape."

Wing asked, "How did he escape?"

Walker smiled. "His escape speaks well of him. His captors kept their prisoners close, watched at night, fed them little, and did not allow them to speak to one another. But they are set to finding, shaping, and moving large stones from a cliffside half a mile away, and that required letting them go back and forth—and, he told me, they had many prisoners and became careless. Kelso watched for days, knew their faces and movements, and knew when they were likely not to see him leave. He saved some of his food for several days; the campsite is a wasteland. He managed to whisper to his leader that he would bring help. Then one day at dusk, when the guards were slack and ready to drink, he slipped away. He ran to the river and saw me there. He's small but fast and tough."

Teller asked, "Is his speech near to ours?"

"Oh, yes," said Walker. "His family is much like yours." He stood and brushed his hands on his tunic. "I don't know him well, but I trust him."

"Thank you, Walker," said Teller. "Now let us tell you the reason for our quest and its origin." He withdrew the stone from his pouch, and they spent the next twenty minutes in conversation.

Walker finally said, "Thank you for putting your trust in me. I will not betray it."

Teller said, "Then let us plan a rendezvous. We are north of the river and have traveled northeast, planning to reach the foothills and follow them east toward the old mountains. Where shall we wait for Kelso?

Walker said, "Go a little south of east from here to rejoin the river. You will find a double bend, from northeast to southeast and back, forested, a pleasant place. Wait there, and Kelso will join you. It will take me three days to return to him, and he will take at least three more to reach you. Take care; large animals sometimes come to the river at that place to drink."

"We will. When will we see you again? And, Walker, why do I trust you so much?"

Walker laughed. "We have both lived many years, and we have learned whom to trust and whom not. Anyway, in this situation you have few friends to choose from. I'll keep an eye on your family prisoners, and I'll see you again before you reach the eastern mountains; it's not yet midsummer."

They spoke their farewells, and Walker slipped away southward.

***

Priam and Tara were alone together in the trees. The calming sound of the river could be heard behind them. They had arrived at the river bend a day ago and were waiting for Kelso. A wish to separate had come over the group after so many days thrown together, traveling, playing their roles in the team. In ones and twos, they had moved quietly apart. These two moved northeast up the river, keeping within its band of trees. They sat together.

Priam had a branch in his hands, a good piece of wood, and was scraping at it with the sharpest stone he could find in the shallow water. But he frowned and shook his head as we worked, then threw down the branch and the stone and stood up, moving his feet restlessly. "We're nowhere," he said.

Tara looked at him intently but did not respond.

"We're nowhere, we have no home, we're stuck out here. No family. I miss my family." He made fists with both hands.

Tara said, "I guess I'm your family now, Priam. And this team is our family."

"I know it. I'm sorry, I was rude." He sat again and stared off into the distance. "We don't really know each other very well." He looked at Tara with a fleeting grin. "We don't have many memories together."

"We're making memories," she replied. "When we are old, these will be precious memories. How we escaped and traveled and found answers and…"

Priam was silent.

"I know you are torn. You want to help your family. Are you sorry you came with us?"

"I love you, Tara, but the rest, I don't know. I don't know what to do, but I want you with me. I want to make memories with you." He touched her knee.

She shivered and said, "Teller warned us not to couple. That was wise, I think. We mustn't hold the others back."

He stood up and grasped both her hands till she rose with him. "Forget the others for just this hour! I need you now, Tara. I want to start those memories now. They will keep me here, satisfy me!"

Tara sighed, and the two made their way deeper into the trees, hand in hand.

26

The land where the river made its double bend was not a gentle plain; its slope steepened, and the ground sank into a valley with fairly steep sides for half a mile or so. In the turn, there was actually a waterfall, only ten or twelve feet high, with an open pool below it. The land broadened beyond the pool as the river slowed and meandered on southward.

They bathed in the waterfall, the first any of them (except Teller) had ever seen. It glittered in the sun, and its coolness, spray, and soft, musical roar were magical. In turn, they stripped and stood in the falling water, shivering and laughing and trying to breathe. Clean and sun-dried, with their tunics on, they rested now within sight of the water and earshot of its low voice. It was warm, and the wind was picking up.

What they were waiting for was the appearance of Kelso. It had now been five days since Walker left them; Kelso should appear soon if nothing bad had happened.

Binta and Stride sat together, apart from the others. They'd both been busy. Stride had walked out, then all the way around their camp, patiently scouting the terrain for hiding places, signs of large animals, and other dangers. Binta had also walked out, hunting for vegetable food and firewood. Now, like the others, they were waiting.

Binta emptied her pouch and began to sort the plants, sniffing them and holding them up to look at the leaves.

"Smell this one," she said and handed a leafy stem to Stride.

He sniffed it, rolled a leaf between his fingers, and sniffed again.

"Whoa, that's nice. And strong. That would make a piece of meat taste fine."

He looked at the other things she had strung out on the grass.

"How did you learn so much about these things?"

"Plants talk to me, in a way. Not with words, but I know them so well, they just seem to tell me by feel and scent who they are."

"Plants are alive, but they've got no speech, no faces. Do you think they have spirits?"

"Oh, I do, plant spirits. And trees talk to us."

"In the wind?"

"No. Their sound is but their stir. They speak by being trees, just letting us touch them."

Stride laughed. "You girls! But you know—sometimes I feel the same way about the animals we hunt. Even that some of them are spirits, or that spirits ride them."

They both smiled and paused.

Binta said, "Priam worries me. He mutters and stares around. Tara doesn't know what to do with him."

Stride said, "He wants to go south to his family. I think he feels that he should. And then he fears doing it. I think he fears both roads. He fears that we will find nothing and come to harm."

He grinned at Binta. "He could be right."

"Do you think so?" said Binta.

"No. He may be right, but that shouldn't stop us. That's what makes it an adventure! And I like our family. Including you."

Binta smiled. "Me too. I'm on your side now, Stride. Sure, we all want to be part of something more. That's what the adventure will bring us to if we win through."

By silent agreement, they walked up closer to the pool, where the others were. Teller had cleared a space of vegetation and was drawing with a stick in the dust, watched by Wing. Ayo also knelt by a cleared circle, but she was spreading out her assortment of leaves, flowers, and berries, sniffing and tasting a fragment of each one, just as Binta had done.

"What have you found?" said Binta, dropping to her knees beside Ayo.

"This might be good," replied Ayo. "The berries are ripe and taste good. These leaves are pretty plump, and these others have a strong aroma and a bitter taste, but somehow, I like them."

"I found some promising roots," said Binta. "Look here—they might be good in hot water if we can manage that again."

She raised her voice. "Stride, we need flesh, a fire, and your bowl. What chances?"

Stride walked over, yawning. "This is an interesting little valley. The smells and signs are different here. The animals are different. There are some footprints on the bank—small furries and one that might be a cat. We might have luck with a sling but at dusk. Can you wait that long?"

"We will if we have to," said Binta. "Can you find a furry sooner? How about fish?"

"I think we've scared the fish away. Maybe Wing and I can go upstream and see what we find."

Stride walked further up, joining Teller and Wing.

"Wing, let's go fishing. What's this?" he said, looking at Teller's drawing.

Wing said, "It's a drawing of where we've been and where we're going. Look here!"

He gestured at the ground, and Teller looked up and sat back on his haunches.

"I drew this so that Wing and I could remember it. East of here's a lot of guesswork, but see, here are the mountains north of us, and far away, they join the mountains in the east, where our destination lies. And south is the country where our families are captive."

They stared at the lines and little mounds. "Is that the river?

"Yes. It's the heart of it. It ties our world together. It starts as a little stream in the eastern mountains, into the big lake, then runs west, picks up other streams, grows and curves south to where we started, and beyond to the Southern Sea. It connects everything."

Stride whistled his appreciation. "You've captured the world in the dust, pretty near. Wing, will you hunt upstream with me? We need to find some supper."

Teller nodded. Wing jumped up, and he and Stride jogged toward the waterfall. They climbed up and around the right of it and disappeared.

***

The sky was still bright in the west, but clouds were thickening northeast of them. The wind became gusty; trees bent their limbs, and a few birds appeared, flying low and calling to one another.

Stride and Wing glided along up the east side of the river above where it dipped into the valley, keeping their shadows clear of the water. Wing had retrieved his net, strong grass ropes tied to a semi-circle of flexible green branch; he held it at both ends.

Stride stopped and pointed. A fish was there, head upstream, tail swishing, poised against the current. Wing nodded, crept carefully to the water's edge, then plunged in straight at the fish, holding the net in front of his chest. A splash, foam, and he stood triumphantly, holding the net closed, the fish inside.

He made his way the few steps toward the shore and held up the net for Stride to grasp. As he raised the net, two strands broke, and the fish disappeared into the water. He looked at the empty net in his hands.

"Damn the spirits! That was a silverfish, enough for all!"

He climbed out, peering at his broken tool.

Wing shook his head resignedly. "I'll weave it again tonight, and use thicker strands." He looked up and around the sky. "It's going to storm. Let's try and catch a furry."

The two young men took small stones out of their belts, spread out and moved quietly through the trees southward into the wind, looking left and right. They stopped and listened and waited. In a few minutes, they heard rustling to their left and moved very slowly in its direction.

A bird fluttered down and landed on a branch above them. Stride straightened up and threw his stone. The bird fell to the ground, and Wing was on it, grasped it, and broke its neck. It was a brown pigeon, sizeable too. He put it into his belt, and they paused again to listen. But the rustling was gone, overcome by the rising wind. And the sun was almost on the horizon.

Stride said, "Let's go back. We need to help with the fire." They started down the slope into the valley. The wind shook the trees harder. A few large drops of rain pelted them, and the air abruptly cooled. They hurried as best they could without tripping. "Fire's gonna have to wait!" Stride grunted.

Ten minutes later, they reached the clearing around the pond. The sky was dark, the wind fierce, the rain pouring down, it was hard even to breathe. A streak of lightning flashed to the ground to their right in a blaze of blinding light, with the snarl of thunder right behind it and the slow crack of a slowly falling tree. As they stumbled back, the tree fell into the pond, and a man appeared out of the gloom, holding his left arm and limping.

27

"Who are you?"

"Kelso. Walker sent me. I'm hurt."

"I'm Stride; this is Wing. Are you followed?

"No."

"Good, then, tell us about your injury." Stride and Wing closed on Kelso and took him each by a shoulder as he drooped with pain and fatigue. "How bad is it?"

Kelso sighed and shook his head. "I fell down the slope above you. The rock gave way. Left arm may be broken; I'm not sure. Left thigh hurts, but I can walk. I'm really glad to see you." He managed a smile.

They clasped hands behind Kelso's lower back and under his thighs, picked him up, and carried him through the blinding rain to the shelter of the trees where the others were waiting out the storm.

The girls cleared a space for him under a tree. Young Aaron scurried about to find him soft underbrush to cushion his back and shoulder. Teller examined him and applied moss to his bleeding scrapes. "I don't think it's broken," he said, "but the shoulder's tender. Let me bind it to your side."

Kelso sat up. He smiled gratefully. Binta brought him water in a small bowl and a few dried herbs for his pain. The storm was easing, and they sat quietly, waiting for the rain to stop and sizing up their new companion. He was gaunt, dark of hair and beard, shorter than the other men and a little older than the young ones, long-headed and brown-eyed. He looked very tired and very relieved.

Teller said, "Kelso, it's good to have you with us. And you said you were not followed, and that's good. But you were certainly in a tearing hurry to get here. Tell us, have you anything urgent to tell us, anything we need to act upon?"

Kelso swallowed and cleared his throat. He frowned with concentration. "I was not followed—I got clear away before they could capture me. And… I never saw them, never believed I was being followed. But I came in haste and without much care to hide my trail."

"So you may be tracked. Do you think it probable?"

"No. Their numbers are not large. And they are very busy now, very occupied with their monument. They always have scouts out looking for more slaves."

"Are the other captives in danger?" asked Priam intently.

Kelso gazed into the distance. "I don't know. Our life was not good there. We were fed badly, whipped to our work, kept quiet mostly. I don't know what they plan for us. They need us for the work, and will for another while. Perhaps we'll be allowed to join their family. But I also heard them speaking of more slave work, and they are ruthless."

Teller said, "Kelso, I am a little confused about the situation down there among the rocks. Will you give us a brief story about your family, how it became entangled with this family that calls itself the Sun Family" and what other tribes are involved either as their partners or their slaves?"

Kelso replied, "I'll do my best. This 'Sun Family' (they used to be the Great Family till they started worshipping the sun) made friends with us several summers ago, coming up from the south. Their leaders were friendly and very talkative, full of questions and stories, and it was some time before we fully realized how different they were. There were more than fifty of them. They had weapons, both wood and stone, and their women had ornaments that they wore in their hair and on their necks. They said they had lived on the sea years ago.

"They surprised us when last summer they called us to a meeting, all of us and all of them, near the Inmost Sea. Their chief told us about their gods and the plan to build a monument to them. Our chief said that we didn't believe in their gods but in the Maker of the old stories. Then their chief asked all of us who did believe in their gods to come to him, strictly voluntarily, no penalty for saying 'no.' And seven men did and three women. Then the rest of us were taken captive in a rush (some killed) and made slaves and marched off to the monument.

"Later, the same thing happened with Ruse's family, except that they were more skillfully lied to, and most of them agreed to join the Great Family's enterprise, remaining a separate tribe. Only a few were made slaves."

"Who were they?" asked Priam.

"I don't know their names," Kelso said. "Three men, two women, a girl." He rocked forward restlessly. "And then, Teller, your family was brought in. And others since. Perhaps twenty, twenty-five of their captor tribes, and four dozen slaves."

"All right," said Teller, "I see it better now. As you see, we are only seven—well, eight with Aaron."

Aaron looked happy.

"We are escaped prisoners, if you will, of the Great and River Tribes, but we are also engaged on a journey which I do not wish to divulge to you until we know each other better. On that journey, we are determined to travel all the way to the eastern mountains. Will you join us?"

"I will, and I thank you joyfully for adopting me. I will be an obedient and helpful companion to you. I do hope that one day you and I will be strong enough to return to our captive tribes and help them to escape."

Binta cried, "We do too." And the rest nodded and gave their comradeship.

28

They stayed at the river bend another five days to prepare their equipment and supplies for a journey across dry plains in hot summer. They had their fraying cloaks, and Ayo and Binta made new tunics from leaves and young branches, tied with grasses, and a few food containers using leaves sewn with wooden needles laboriously sharpened on rough rock. The rest gathered food, both vegetable and animal whatever they could find and kill, birds, fish, small animals. No larger animals were at hand in this season, and anyway, the group felt themselves not strong enough to tackle a wolf or giant cat. They longed to have a chance at a large leaf-eater, not only for the meat but also to skin it for new cloaks and carry-alls.

Kelso was especially good at making things, and he had a few tools beyond the usual wooden mallet and sharp stones. What he called a "sword" was a bar nearly as long as his forearm made of a dark gray hard, glassy substance with a very sharp edge on one side of it, made, he said, by hours of patient rubbing against the hardest stone he could find. It was the best cutting tool any of them had seen. He could cut and shape wood, sever reeds and grasses, and even cut his and the others' hair—better than the grind of using stones. He'd kept it hidden from his captors.

In the evening, they invented and played another game—the old tree-ball game suffered from a lack of the right trees. In this one, played in the meadow, one team of three (Stride, Binta, Ayo) defended a stone placed in the center of a circle fifteen paces across, with the other team (Priam, Wing, Tara) circling and throwing the ball to one another; the first player to have a clear throw at the stone took it. Hit, and you scored; miss, and the other team "took the field." There was much running and laughter and some contact. The third time in, Stride's team defended Priam and Wing well but let Tara slip open. She scooped up a low pass from Wing and bounced it off the stone triumphantly.

"We won! Bring us a drink!" she cried as they walked back to the river.

"This is slave-taking," grumbled Stride, and he and Ayo filled the wooden bowl from the lake. Teller added an aromatic liquor from a precious stone bottle, and they passed it around.

"Oh-wa," Kelso uttered on his taste. "What is that stuff?"

"We call it brandy," Teller said. "You boil wine a little, it gets stronger."

Ayo pointed to a great flight of birds high above as they wheeled together to the north.

"What a beautiful place! I could build a tent here. We talked about spirits today. I feel good ones here, a blessed place. 'The Falls.'"

"Maybe we'll see it again," said Wing.

Now, the plan was to make progress in the morning and the evening, when the air was cool and the sun low, sleep in darkness, and rest or mend during the middle day. They would follow the river until it turned north, then strike east to the foothills and follow them to a rumored inland lake where the water was fresh. Going across the dry plain from water to water would be a challenge.

They rose before the sun. When it first appeared, it was north of east and climbed its arc nearly straight up. No clouds, wind out of the north, a glorious summer day, and they began. Stride led as before, keeping the river on his left. Teller stayed in the center with the girls, who, along with Aaron, were carrying most of their supplies. Priam and Wing moved out on their right flank, scouting for threats and opportunities. Wing brought up the rear.

There didn't seem to be cause for silence. Ayo hummed a melody, then several took it up with old known words, a marching song with a good walking beat. When the song was over, a couple of them kept on humming quietly.

They eased away from the river as they strode, keeping it in sight with its brush and clumps of trees; such shelter would be welcome when they stopped. But travel was faster out in the open. It was scrub grass, less than knee-high, dry ground but always with occasional insects and one pale-brown leg-long snake scurrying away. Then the grass well ahead of them moved with the movement of a bushy-tailed animal, then another. Too small to stop and hunt. But animals like those, hunters of smaller life, were always the prey of larger. There was a flash of wings, and a bird made a sharp pullout and flew away with the rat in its claws.

As the sun neared its apex above and south of them, Stride moved gradually closer to the river, aiming for a distant group of trees. In an hour, they were there and ready for camp. Teller stuck an upright stick as long as his arm in the ground and stuck a smaller stick right on the tip of its shadow. The others prepared food and water.

"Tell us about your family," said Teller to Kelso as they hunkered down to their meal. "What is its ancient history? What do you know of this Maker of whom I spoke and his silence?"

Kelso sat silent for a minute, rocking back and forth gently. "I am not a Teller," he said, "and I don't know the stories well. But my family sees spirits in many places: in the forest trees, in the river waters, and in the day sky and the night sky. What we don't understand about the world, they understand. We think they walk about among us, disguised as animals or even birds, judging how we live and punishing us for evil. We call them gods.

"There are stories of an old Maker, and how He made the forest, and how he fought an enemy who caused us to be evil. I don't know whether these things are true. We don't worship this older Maker—we don't see him or hear his voice. We try to live in harmony with the half-seen Makers of the earth and sky. We pray mostly to the sun spirit and the river spirit."

"Are there any stories of our first Father and Mother?"

"None that I remember," said Kelso.

"How does your leader explain the evil in some people?"

"We seldom talk of such things."

Teller nodded thoughtfully, stood up, and returned to his stick in the ground. Its shadow had moved, and he placed another stone at the tip of the new shadow. He drew a line in the dirt with a stick, stone to stone and longer. He knew that this line marked East and West, the points on the horizon where the sun rose and fell in spring and fall. He looked at the river and the far-off hills, back to the line, again to the river and the hills.

"The river is still trending northeast. Let's follow it for now. When it turns north, we turn east, straight to the eastern mountains."

Stride nodded.

29

They continued northeast along the river, mostly in the trees, sometimes in the open. Clouds built up, a shower wetted them, and the sun reappeared farther west. As it grew nearer to setting, turning the western sky gold-orange, another grove of trees was visible in the distance, and they decided to walk to these for their night's rest.

After washing, building a fire, and eating, the group broke up into two, the men moving down to the water and the women staying by the fire. They chatted separately.

"How are supplies, everyone?" Teller asked the young men.

Wing responded, "It's beautiful high summer—we don't need a lot. We'll need more food in five days or so. Water? Depends on the route we take. Enough for now."

Stride added, "It'll be colder when we reach the mountains. We're going to need new capes—and sandals, maybe. And time and vines to re-strengthen our packs."

Priam and Kelso were silent. Priam was frowning. Teller wondered what they were thinking but sensed that this was not the time to ask.

In the women's group, Tara was saying, "We're running a little low on grains and leaves for the food, and I'd like more for the medicine bag, too, just in case."

Binta replied, "The plants are different here. They may not have the best ones. I hope we find some of the healing ones."

"Yes… we'll have to keep sampling and smelling and hope we do."

Ayo had been looking down at the men. "I was thinking about what Kelso said and why some of us are evil."

"If Teller's story is right," answered Tara, "it came after that first quarrel with the Maker. I wonder why Kelso's family has forgotten that."

Ayo pondered. "Well, the story doesn't say what happened, just that suddenly He left us. But it's true; there's some evil in all of us. We have to fight it, push it down."

Tara frowned. "I wish the Maker would talk to us about that. We don't know what to do, and He's silent."

Dark fell with no moon, and they slept. The fire became red coals, then gray, and went cold.

It was still dark but cooler when Stride's eyes opened to a noise. He remained still and listened. It was a sound of movement north of him, brush and branches, not loud but not stealthy either. Then there was a low animal grunt and another answering. He turned, rose, and put his hand on each sleeper's shoulder, one by one, with a "Hush!" each time. They all sat up and listened. The sounds grew louder.

Stride whispered, "It's a herd, maybe antelopes. Let's hunt them—we need meat and hides!"

"To the trees, with stones and spears."

Now, there was a rustle of human motion as objects were sought and found.

Kelso limped to Stride's ear and whispered, "I have a rope loop; I'll try it if it gets light enough."

Stride nodded. There was gray dawn in the east. He whispered to the women.

"Tara, up with us. Binta, Ayo, circle south; herd them to us if they move that way."

In thirty seconds, all was quiet again, except for the light movements of the deer. The waiting had begun.

The darkness was turning to gray. Trees began to become visible.

Teller did not climb a tree with the others. He moved quietly near the remains of the fire and picked up his precious pack, then moved back to the bank of the river to wait in reserve. The team had done this hunting many times before when the family was intact; they assumed their roles without orders.

In nearby trees were Stride, Wing, Priam, and Tara, armed with stones and short spears. Kelso, with a bad left arm and not a climber, was behind the trunk of the tree nearest the fire. He had his lasso, made of long, tough strands of vine, and a weapon with no name, a short stout wooden stick with a heavy rock securely tied into its notched end.

It was not very long, perhaps ten minutes, until the leaders of the herd were among them, moving toward the river to drink. There was enough light now to see shapes. Stride hissed. The animals stopped, ears forward. And down came a small shower of hurled stones.

Unhurt antelopes ran. Two hurt ones were down. The team dropped from their trees, wrestled with the two, and killed them expertly with spears. At the same time, Kelso threw his loop over an antelope's neck with his good arm. Both he and the antelope fell as he pulled it in. Teller helped him kill it, and they had three fine animals to feed them and clothe them.

"What a piece of work!" exclaimed Teller. "You are a splendid team. Let's rest for a few minutes, then do our work quickly so that nothing will spoil. Be on watch for scavengers; the smell will be everywhere."

"No need to rest," cried Binta. "Is anyone injured? No? Let's get the fire going again." She and Wing tackled it. Aaron ran off to gather wood.

Teller and Ayo took one prize, Stride and Wing the second, Priam and Tara the third. The animals were skinned, the meat stripped off and laid out on gathered sticks to dry. Tendons and bladders were removed and cleaned for other uses. While Binta took the largest cuts and set them out to cook, the others began the important and time-consuming work of cleaning and scraping the hides. When dried, they would be smeared with fat and made supple for new capes and sandals.

Priam was scraping his hide. His stone wasn't sharp and kept slipping; his hands and arms were greasy. He threw down the stone and stood up.

"I'm a hunter, not a bloody tailor!"

Tara looked up. "You look pretty bloody this morning, dear man."

Priam looked down at himself in disgust.

"This whole expedition is too much. We've taken on too much for the few of us. Winter's going to come, and we'll be out here all alone to starve and freeze. It's going to fail." He looked off at the others. "And there's too much of this good-and-evil nonsense!"

Tara came and touched his shoulder.

"You're just tired, hot, and frustrated. Have a drink, cool off in the water. We'll be fine."

She went back to her work, not feeling very well herself. She had little appetite for the meat Wing was roasting.

30

It took six days of hard work to finish, but the job was done. All the backpacks had been strengthened and re-sewn. Stride carried an additional pack low on his back filled with almost-dried meat (it would be put out to dry during mid-day break until it was ready.) Wing and Priam each carried in the same way the hides to be worked on each evening till they were supple and ready to be cut. Two older leather bags were cleaned, double-sewn and ready to be filled with water for their trek. There'd be evaporation and a little leakage, but they would hold for three or four days.

They had discussed building a sledge with runners made from curved branches stripped of their bark, to carry the food and hides. But they decided it would take too long and might not hold up in the rough country that would be coming.

They did contrive a rude sun shelter for their midday breaks—stout sticks to push into the ground and spread hides over for a lean-to.

Next daybreak, there was a last meal of fresh meat and greens, and the fire was covered with dirt. Packs were donned in an atmosphere of quiet tension; the future now was truly unknown. Off they went at a good pace set by Stride, not as fast as when they traveled lighter. The more heavily burdened still kept to the center; the men went wide as scouts and lookouts. The ground was dry, and the sky was dead clear. The river, narrower and noisy, was still on their left.

They halted at noon for food and rest, setting up the lean-to and putting meat strips on it to dry. Teller stuck his stick in the ground, pondered the length of the shadow, and called his people together.

"Look," he said, "My stick's shadow grew shorter all spring. Then it stopped shortening; that was when Walker told us about Kelso; it had been the same for three days. That meant we were at the longest day. Midsummer was here twenty days ago. The shadow is getting longer now, and every morning, you will see the sun rising a little later and farther south."

Wing asked, "How far have we come? How far to go?"

Teller smiled. "If only I knew. But we are heading for the Eastern Mountains, and we can't even see them yet. Walking, I think we make ten or fifteen miles a day. We stop and forage every several days—we have to. If I put nine times ten pebbles in a tiny sack and threw one out each night, we might—just might—reach our goal before the last one was gone."

Stride spoke thoughtfully. "What dangers do you see ahead of us?"

"Animals and thirst, first of all," Teller replied. "Later, sickness and starvation. I don't fear human enemies west of the mountains. In the mountains, who knows? But my hope is for allies instead."

Tara chimed in. "I have herbs for some sicknesses, but we are short of them. I hope to find more along the route, Teller; can you plan it that way?"

"Again, dear Tara, I wish I knew."

Ayo said, "This may sound foolish since the Maker has been so silent for so long. But if this is a good pilgrimage, he will watch over us. I feel Him sometimes. Sometimes, I even talk to Him, ask for our needs. I never hear an answer."

Binta said, "I do that too."

Priam said, "Only humans can protect humans."

Kelso said, "My family would pray to the local gods we believe have power over the sun and the storms and the rivers. Our Teller was a special man who knew what to say to them. His prayers made all of us feel safer."

Teller said, "I have had all these different thoughts. I don't know whether the Maker will keep storms from us or bring us to water. The water runs where He puts it. But I do know that asking Him to help us decide what to do is good."

"So, goodness comes from the Maker?" asked Tara.

"It seems to me," said Ayo, "that goodness is both in us and outside us. Goodness exists whether we're good or not. It's like the moon; everybody can see it."

After a little more talk, they lay under the lean-to and slept.

After sleep came relief, a drink from the river, and back on the march. The sun was well past the zenith now, but they still had four hours clear to make progress. There was less urgency in marching now, less sense of possible trouble.

When the sun reached the trees behind them, they stopped, prepared supper, and ate. When they had finished, Teller said, "Now Kelso, are you ready to hear of our quest and why we are on this journey?"

"Ready and aching to know," said Kelso.

Teller reached into his pouch and pulled out the stone. "This is what started it all," he said. "In the history of our family, it was given to our first leader when men broke up and one family became many. It was said then that the Maker gave it to the father as they were leaving the garden . He told them it would permit them to turn speech into symbols that could be turned back into speech back from the stone—writing, he called it. After the father and the mother had left the garden, somehow, it broke into pieces. This piece came to us, and I do not know the fate of the other pieces, just that there was at least one other. No one since has been able to understand the stone.

"I have always thought that the other pieces might be found if we returned to the garden and looked for them. And I have imagined with longing being able to carve the history of our family—maybe of all the tribes— on stones, instead of relying on memory. I am growing old, and these, my young friends and students, saw the value of the quest and its excitement, and we decided to try it. Our planning was nearly finished when our family was attacked at our spring camp, and we quickly gathered together and fled. Since then we have felt some remorse at not going to the aid of our captured family. But we were too few; we would just have become captives ourselves. We decided to continue our quest, try to find allies, and return by a southern route to see if we could help them escape. We are still too few now to fight such evil. And you are our first recruit."

He handed the stone to Kelso, who looked at it with intense curiosity, front and back. "It's glass, I think, a kind of melted rock I've seen before. It seems to have symbols scratched into it by a harder rock."

"Yes. Most of the symbols are quite simple, lines and circles. There are about sixteen of that kind. See, all eighteen are put in a single column. Then below, they are repeated, mixed up in groups of three or more. Now, on the other side, instead of simple marks repeated, are curved figures; some look like an attempt at pictures. Not many; the broken stone left little room. We've not figured out what it all means."

"I suppose another family got the other pieces," Wing said wistfully.

"Perhaps," said Teller. "But I have a hope that they might be found still in the original place. Guarded, even."

"Guarded!" Stride whistled. "By friends or enemies?"

"Well, it's a dangerous journey," Teller smiled. "Whatever happens will be a surprise."

31

The days were hot, the terrain was getting rough, and going was slow. The strain was showing on the travelers; there was less laughing and singing and occasional flares of temper. The land east of the river was no longer a gentle plain. It was beginning to rise and fall like waves of soil, making a jumble of gentle ridges and valleys.

After several days, the river bent left toward the rocky hills in the north. It was shallower and thinner, merely a stream now—their precious water was less. That was when Teller, consulting with Stride and Binta, decided the time had come to strike east. They still had plenty of food. They bathed gingerly in the now-colder waters, drank their fill, then filled their leather water sacks and sewed them again against leaks. Water was their worry. But they believed they would move faster in the plain than in the hills.

In the evenings, Teller returned to his old practice of reciting some of the family's history. The youths not native to his family—Priam, Binta, and especially Kelso, needed to hear it, he thought, to understand the journey better. And Wing needed to hear it again and again, against the time when he would be the Teller of his tribe.

"The father and the mother lived long, and by the time they died, the tribe had grown to more than a hundred people. They divided themselves into families, of course; those of Cain and Seth, their sons, and of their daughter Elanor. A son, Abel, had died. For another lifetime, they stayed close together for hunting, protection, and friendship. But jealousies arose, sometimes about small slights, sometimes about bigger things like leadership and even different memories of their parents and grandparents.

Teller turned and looked at Wing. "My student, you have heard this from me many times. Test yourself; tell us the rest."

Wing stared at Teller briefly. He wiped his hands on the dry ground. Then he stared into space, rehearsing. In a flat voice that was hoarse for a moment, he said,

"One spring, Seth's grandson, Cainan, wanted to move the family onto the unknown plains to the west. The summers were colder then, and the cold winds coming down the mountain carried more rain. But the grandsons of Cain, Irad and Priam (your namesake, Priam), were determined to move to the south and east, where more land beckoned. Arguments were given, but past hurts and present resentments were spoken and then shouted. It ended in the withdrawal of the parties to their own family clearings. On the day after a great storm blew down trees and destroyed tents, three families set out on their separate journeys. Summer journeys had always happened. But this time, no one (save for a few) would return to the forests near the garden."

Teller said, "Well done. We are the descendants of the Family of Seth."

Priam asked Kelso, "Is this the same story your Teller tells?"

Kelso was sitting with elbows on knees, chin in his hands. He raised his head and said, "Parts are the same, and parts are different. Our Tribal Father was Cain—Haem, we call him—and our story tells very little about his father and mother. Just that he was betrayed by Abel, and his family traveled south and east to find peace beyond the mountains."

Binta said, "Priam and I heard something like that version. That blood had been spilled, and the old enmity never healed over till the breach. But that was so long ago. Does it matter now?"

Teller said, "It only matters if we carry the hurt in our hearts."

Priam responded, "So you think we should forget the past."

Teller shook his head. "No, never! I would not have spent years rehearsing the exact words of these stories if I thought them unimportant, Priam. We must remember our history and try very hard to keep it true. If we suffered past wrongs, we must not forget them. We must just forgive them. So that we can remember all the way back to our common purpose."

In the predawn darkness, miles to the south, Walker and his dog saw a vague shadow moving across the plain. He followed silently until he could identify it as a man, traveling fast with his head down. He sighed, shook his head, and turned back east, following the searchers.

In the morning, they could not find Priam.

He had settled for sleep with the others. But his cloak and pack were gone. No one had heard him leave. The eight split up and walked slowly around the perimeter of their camp. Ayo called, "Here, I think these are his footprints." She was to the south of the camp. The others looked, and Stride managed to follow the impressions for a hundred feet before they disappeared. No one could see anything of him in the distance. They returned to the camp and looked at one another, and at Tara, and at Teller.

Teller said, "He is a troubled boy. Talented but troubled. I believe he never quite felt loyal to our quest. Tara, you are betrothed to him. What do you think is happening?"

Tara walked back and forth, hands clutching elbows. "You're right, Teller, he had doubts, he missed his family, he found fault with you, with us. He swore he loved me, and…" She shook her head. "I am furious."

"Perhaps he will walk off his confusion and return. He knows our direction. I'm afraid that searching for him would be futile. Let us continue to the east."

They completed their meal and chores and packed up for the day—mostly in silence and short words. This was a blow to their strength and, most of all, their confidence. But Teller would not let them dwell on it now. Everyone needed to be tired and sweaty. Stride led them out toward the rising sun at a fast pace.

In the evening, when the young people were hard at their chores, it was Teller's habit to take a walk away from the group, not far, in case one or more of them wanted a private conversation. This evening, Tara approached him and stood beside him silently.

Teller said, "This running away is a terrible blow for you."

Tara said, "Yes. I am with child."

Teller nodded. "I know, dear Tara. I have seen the signs for several days. Did Priam know?"

"I did not tell him."

"Well, your child will be one of our family. We will all be its fathers. It will be difficult in the cold, but we are used to it being difficult. We wouldn't know how to behave if life were easy."

She put her hands on his shoulders and embraced him briefly. "I will tell the others tomorrow," she said. Then, "I am very alone."

Tara walked back to the group, Teller remaining behind. As she drew near, Ayo and Binta rose and approached her. Binta gestured with her hand to walk aside, away from the men. Then she said, "We know you are with child, Tara."

Tara glanced at them, then looked down, touching her abdomen.

Ayo said, "I don't think the men know it yet. But—don't worry. We'll be your sisters and birth-helpers."

Tara said, "Oh, friends. I am so angry—with myself. I should have listened to Teller. I've just made things harder for you, for all of us. I'll be a drag on the family, on the whole expedition."

Binta touched both her shoulders. "No, you won't; you're too tough to fall behind. We'll take care of the boys.... Oh, how can he have run? I thought he was good."

Tara shook her head. "In the end, no... I was fooled."

Ayo said, again, "Good is both in us and outside of us." She touched Tara briefly. "Maybe Priam will see it soon."

After a silence, Tara said, softly, "I'll tell them in the morning. Then we can plan how to go along."

Three foreheads leaned together and touched.

***

During the night, cold rain pushed through; it was colder and a strong wind came out of the north. They did not normally make a fire in the morning—it took too long—and they didn't this morning either. But they wrapped their robes closer as they broke their fasts.

Tara spoke. "My brothers and sisters, you must know that Priam and I did not take Teller's advice. We coupled, and I am with child."

She looked into each pair of eyes.

"But I am still loyal to you and to our quest. I am sorry for what I have done because it may make the quest more difficult. But I am committed to its success, and I will do everything in my power not to hold you back if you will keep me."

Stride looked at her, nodded, and asked, "Did Priam know of the child?"

"I didn't tell him. But I drew away from him after I was sure, and he may have guessed."

"I await a word with him when he tries to walk back into our family."

Teller said, "I know you're angry, Stride. But we must be judges, not revenge-takers. If we meet again, we'll hear his story and consult with Tara before we decide anything."

"Of course." Stride spat. "To you, Tara, I promise that we will help you with all our strength. You are our sister."

Wing said, "I am with you too." And Kelso nodded.

"Well said," said Teller. "Now, drink from the bowls we set out last night, all of it. We may not see water again this day."

They set out walking, bent against the wind and rain. The valley they were in was wide, the grass knee-high, flattened by occasional faint trails. Stride and Wing scanned the horizon every few minutes, looking for signs of movement. There were none.

"I wonder when we'll come to trees and water again," said Wing.

Stride responded, "I think we'll cross a tributary spring in a few days. We should begin to see foothills in the north about then and rejoin the river in… ten or twenty days, I guess. Then, we follow it eastward, where the mountains will eventually appear. Stay north of the Great Lake, Walker said. The garden is in those mountains. Thirty more days? Forty? Cold will be starting."

Wing looked around again. "This is still antelope country, and that means tiger country. I hope we reach the mountains before they get hungry."

"And before we run out of food and water," said Stride. But he didn't say it glumly. Stride was an optimist.

32

An east wind was blowing and it bore a thin, persistent rain down on the place where Elwin and his fellow captives were being held.

They numbered over a hundred now. Their camp was half a mile east of the hill where a great monument was being erected. It was near the place where an outcropping of sandstone provided the stones for the monument. There were no trees at all; the only shelter was from crevices in the outcropping itself; only grasses were growing there. Water was from a stream that meandered its way east to west half a mile north of the hill. So the camp was rude and filthy. The prisoners had agreed on a place east of the camp to relieve themselves, but the guards wouldn't allow them to go far, so the smell was always present.

The majority of them were men, and to them was given the job of cutting, smoothing, and hauling the stones. These were huge flat things, about as long as a man, half as wide as one, and as thick as a man's arm. They were marked for size in the rock of the outcropping, then the marks deepened into crevices with stone hammers and chisels, then sharpened lengths of hard wood hammered into the crevices until the rock broke free. It was smoothed and flattened (at least on the side facing up) and prepared for hauling.

With no wheels and no beasts of burden, men had to provide the muscle power for a task that seemed impossible. But it was done. One end of the stone was levered up enough to insert a rounded log across its end, then another, then another. Then the other end was lifted and placed on these rollers. Then stout ropes of the strongest vines that could be found were looped around a short crosspiece, and both ends of the rope were taken up by as many men as possible, at least three ropes and thirty men.

The path to the hill was smoothed by hand and chisel as much as possible, and dozens of logs—hauled from trees west of the Great River, all the same diameter, as close as they could manage—arranged in front of the stone. It took days just to prepare to haul one stone half a mile and days to do the hauling. Sometimes, three different teams were hauling three stones to the Temple. Ropes gave way, feet were crushed, and sometimes, a rock would crack and split, ruining it.

You can imagine that it was not a pleasant camp. The men from the south were giving the orders to the forced laborers—"begars" they were called—and striking them with their "chawbucks," large wooden whips. There was a meal of roots and bread at daybreak, work with water breaks, and another meal at sunset. The name of the hill was Mithra-Koh.

It was evening now, and Elwin and his fellow captives were sitting in the darkness. They could talk a little because most of the guards were off eating and drinking, and the ones left were anxious for their turn.

Elwin turned to Artisan. Softly, he said, "How ever can we escape from here?"

Artisan was not a philosopher. He was a man who worked with his hands and his tools and solved problems. So he didn't laugh or groan at Elwin's question. He paused, chewing on a chunk of potato, then said, "The first job would be getting past the guards. I haven't decided when the best time would be—now or just before sunrise, when they're at their most careless. But it depends on which guards are there. Watch them; some are energetic, some lazy. Some are cruel, a few mild. Some could be overcome by a rush, others are too strong. Pick a night with the right guards watching."

Elwin pondered. "How many of us could go at once?"

"I'd say all who are healthy and can move fast."

"Should we recruit from other families?"

"Yes, surely, we'll need the strength—but I leave the picking to you. I'll give you my opinions. Ask Gratia, too, about the women. One traitor in on our plans, and it's death to us all."

"True," said Elwin. "Now, once free of the guards, how and where do we run?"

"Back the way we came is my first thought. West to the river and up. Away from people."

Elwin thought. "Let's think about this. You know…it's going to be much harder than it seems to us now."

They settled in to sleep.

The next night, Elwin moved closer to the group where the women sat for their meal. He spotted Gratia but waited until the guard on that side moved away; then he signaled her. She looked about carefully, waited, then rose and came to him. They spoke in whispers.

"How are you, my love?" he asked.

She looked at him with repressed fury. "Did you see Diss walking guard tonight? Bold, strutting, boasting loudly with his friends. Drunk, probably. I want to kill him for killing my friends. Lying to us. Exile indeed! Him and Ruse. I would die gladly in the task. It would be plain justice."

"So it would," Elwin agreed. "But a greater satisfaction might be possible."

"How could that be?"

"Artisan and I are trying to imagine an escape. The guards are fewer than we are and becoming careless. We might be able to overcome them and run."

"Who are the 'we'?"

"That's just the question. We need to decide which prisoners can be trusted with the plan, which might rise and fight with us in the moment—and which would run to our captors to raise them up."

"Ah," she said. "That's the risk in it. If our numbers were overwhelming… well, I can tell you that some of these women would fight with us to the death. Most of the rest would join us once they saw what was happening. But there are two or three… we would have to deal with."

Elwin whispered, "I thought you would know, and I rejoice in you." He put his hand on her shoulder. "Stane's wife died giving birth, as you know. The pain does lessen."

She looked down but briefly placed her hand on his. "How urgent is it to decide?"

"Not urgent. Slow and very careful. Tell no one yet. But I will tell Abel, get him thinking."

Gratia nodded and made to arise and return to the women. But she stopped, kneeling, when she saw the turtle dove. He appeared out of the darkness, wings spread for landing. And instead of landing before them, he landed softly on Gratia's left shoulder. She turned her head toward him; he stroked her cheek gently with his head, then took off in a flutter of wings and flew away.

Elwin put his hand where Gaby had landed, and they watched him disappear.

33

Slubgob was at the Monument—actually in a copse west of it. He was accompanied by Ruse and Diss, and they were facing a cold, distant Satan, his face immobile.

Satan leaned forward. In a quiet, smooth voice, he said, "Is this what you call moving carefully, arousing no suspicions, gaining their confidence?"

Ruse cleared his throat. "Honorable Leader, there was sudden opportunity and no time. We were sure that our success would so forward your aims that our haste would be praised." He glanced at his colleagues. "Adam's Tribe, basically, is no more. A handful of prisoners and a few who fled and may die in the arid plains. And you will have your temple to defy the Maker."

Satan looked at Slubgob. "What do you have to say?"

Slubgob bowed his head, avoiding eye contact. "I exceeded my authority. I regret doing so. I hope that the outcome is pleasing to you and will forward your work—and that you will forgive me and trust me in the future." There was sweat on his forehead.

Satan spoke to all three, almost in a whisper. "We are an army engaged in a great and long war, with death the prize of the loser. Obedience, absolute obedience, is necessary. Your actions, even if they succeed, as they seem to be doing, will require our strategy to be changed.

"You are all within a mistake of death." He turned away and vanished.

When Satan had rejoined his counselors, he outlined the situation and asked for comments.

Belial grunted. "They took military action and succeeded. Killing other men. Yes, it was beyond their instructions. But it was a good piece of work."

Beelzebub scratched his large, bald head. "Let's think how the situation has changed. We thought to corrupt Adam's family and use it to hasten the corruption of others. We have both gained and lost. What other tribe should we turn our attention to?"

"Is it time to pay attention to those humans who remain on the mountain near Eden?" Mammon mused.

Satan said, "They've been isolated and harmless for a long time. But this visit by the Adam's remnant, if they get there, might awaken them, make them a danger. And yes, possibly an opportunity."

Moloch broke in. "We have a cave there, near the big lake. They specialize in entrapping passersby and spreading fear, don't they? Could they help?"

Satan: "They're worth a visit. Take care of that, will you, Mammon? And Belial, keep a close eye here on the temple, till the monument is finished and the slaves disposed of. There are still some malcontents there worth watching."

34

There was no water.

And there was very little food. The plain went on, monotonous, unchanging. The rain stopped at midday, and though the north wind continued to blow, the ground showed signs of long drought; it was cracked and dry, with sparse grass and few plants worth chewing. Often, a plain like this would teem with life. But this summer, there was none in sight. The travelers licked drops of water from their robes.

They slept close together but with no fire (no trees, no fuel), no leaves to lie on, and no protection against nocturnal meat-eaters. At least the nights were quiet. Wing lay on his side. When he licked his lips, he could taste the salty dust under him. It tasted vaguely of animals and plants and made him hungry.

He turned onto his back and stared. The stars were there in their hundreds. Every few minutes, a bright streak flashed across the night sky. As a student of Teller, he had learned the names of a few of the bright stars and of the groups into which they divided, named for great animals and gods, wheeling slowly westward. They move to the west, and each night ,they rise imperceptibly earlier so that the sight at midnight changes with the seasons. The Old Lion would rise soon, with his bright shoulders and thin waist, with the Lioness trailing after. When he saw them, Wing thought of Walker, trailed by his faithful dog. A stranger had once said to him, "The stars control everything." Walker didn't see how that could be true. But Wing wondered.

The days went on, and low hills to the north appeared and drew a little closer, but there was still no sign of mountains in the east. Their water was gone on the sixth evening. They conferred.

"This is our dilemma," Teller said. "Shall we turn north for the hills, hoping to find a stream there, or keep going east, hoping to cross a tributary flowing north towards the river?"

Wing said, "We left the river behind many days ago. It may be far north of us; the hills may be dry. I say go east."

Stride snorted impatiently. "Let's look around us. It's parched, treeless. It goes on east as far as we can see, the same. We can't see the eastern mountains. There are no birds and no animals. I say turn north."

Binta spoke with suppressed intensity. "Early this morning, I thought I heard lowing, very faintly, to the north. Did anyone else hear that?"

Ayo cried, "I did, and yesterday at sunset, birds flew above us, very high, going that way."

Wing persisted. "This ground is becoming steeper. If the river is north, there must be streams ahead flowing from it. There were rounded pebbles in the swale yesterday."

Stride: "You long for the eastern mountains, young brother. It clouds your sight."

Wing: "What do you long for, Stride? What we left behind?"

Stride: "And you? Does what we seek even exist? I heard Elwin say once, 'If you don't know where you're going, you'll never get there.'"

Tara had listened silently. Now she spoke. "My mouth is dry, and my skin is wrinkled. And so are we all, with thirst. We must head for the nearest water lest we die. I would even say return, go west to the river, if we thought we could live to reach it."

Stride said, "I will admit a great mistake, and beg your pardon for it, going east. But no more, no more!" Stride and Wing stood facing one another with angry faces.

Teller rose, slowly, and looked around the circle. "Hardship and fear clash with eagerness and hope. It was a joint decision to go east. But the signs seem to point north. I wish Walker had told us more about this desert."

The tension diminished. They all sat down, thinking. Teller asked, "Have any of us seen animal signs at all? Any traces of herds?"

This time, it was Kelso who spoke. "Two days ago, droppings, tight and dried. To the left of us. I didn't look north or south. But I haven't seen them since."

Teller said, "All right. What evidence we have points toward the star that doesn't move. Let us turn in that direction. We are not abandoning our quest, Wing—we're just postponing it so that we may live. Will you all agree?" There were nods. All arose and took formation, Stride in the lead, going north.

Walker was coming closer to them as they thought of him.

He had ventured far south in the fading summer, following Priam distantly, finally approaching the Monument where some of Priam's family were jailers and some were prisoners. He stayed out of sight, approaching closely during the night only, using his dog as a scout to warn him of nearby danger. His aim was to get close enough to overhear some conversation, to discover Priam's reception, and perhaps even to have a word with someone from Elwin's family.

Priam's plan had been different. He approached the Monument from the north in evening daylight, and as soon as he could see movement, he called out, "Hello. This is Priam from the River Family! I am your friend!"

Within minutes, he was surrounded by three guards armed with spears. He raised his hands in friendship and said, "I am of the family of Ruse and his men. I was kidnapped by the Adam's

Family people who escaped. I have escaped from them myself and can tell of them!"

He paused and looked at them. They looked at him, too, without greeting or expression. Then they held a whispered discussion, and their leader (the oldest and fattest) said, "Come with us." One of them felt beneath Priam's cloak and looked at his bundle. Then they set off, two beside and one ahead, making for the Monument.

Walker, from the ditch to the north, couldn't hear the words, but saw the action. He settled himself to wait for darkness.

As they approached the Monument, the prisoners were lifting another stone into its place. The task required days of strength and patience. Wedging the flat stone exactly into place, tilting it upward with ropes and many men till it leaned against its already-erected base. Then raising the bottom of it with levers and with ropes guided over tall tree-trunk pillars, a few inches at a time, sliding stones into the gap so gained. A mistake would break the stone and probably result in the execution of a prisoner or two.

Elwin, working with the others, saw Priam entering the area and recognized him. He thought Priam would not remember him, but he instinctively turned his back. Priam was escorted around the perimeter of the work site and on to the south, where the Sun Family leaders had their camp. He was brought to the only tree, at whose base their leader kept his cloak. The guards held his arms firmly.

The leader was sitting on a large stone carved with images, sharpening a knife. He looked up at the group silently.

"Strut, we captured this youth entering the Monument from the north. He claims to be a friend."

Strut stood and faced Priam. "Release him," he said. The guards stepped back. "Tell me who you are and why you have come here."

"My name is Priam," he stammered. "My family is the River Family. I was taken away when they captured the men of Adam's Family and brought them here. Ruse will vouch for me."

"Tell Ruse to come here." An assistant went off, and Strut resumed his sharpening. When Ruse came, he indicated Priam to him and asked, "Is this person yours? Is he to be with us or a prisoner?"

Ruse looked at Priam. Priam bowed, tilting his head up to look at Ruse, and grinned. "Oh, Ruse, it is good to see you again!"

"You were betrothed to that girl from Adam's Family. You ran off when we attacked. You were besotted with her. Why are you here?"

"I didn't know about the attack. Ruse, I had promised the girl in your presence. We were meeting to plan a journey when you attacked—and I was not told. Then we went so far… but I realized I belonged here, with my family, with you. I can tell you where they are, where they are going, what they have."

Ruse turned to Strut. "His story is true, as far as it goes. He may be made a prisoner or not. We need to question him to decide. It would be useful to know where those runaways have gone."

Strut said, "Question him. Find out all he knows. Then bring him back to me." He went back to his knife.

That evening, Walker crept closer to the prison area to observe and listen. From behind a mound of rubble, he saw that the prisoners loosely divided themselves into groups, mostly sticking with members of the same family. Carefully, he scanned the faces he could see. There was a group of prisoners from the River Family, and Priam was with them. His interview must have gone badly.

And there was a group from Adam's Family. Walker recognized Elwin and Gratia. But he had not met or spoken to either of them. The only one who might recognize him was a young man from his old family, the Inmost Sea Family, who had left to adventure for a year and was found in trouble by Walker, who had helped him to survive, and encouraged his return. His name was Lingo. Yes, there he was.

Walker had thought carefully along the way about how to contact a prisoner. A mistake could lead to being a prisoner himself and one possibly subjected to interrogation and torture. He had to somehow separate his contact from the group and always to have an escape route. And he had noticed where the men and women went to relieve themselves.

Taking his time, he worked his way around the northern boundary to the east, then south, looking always for guards, and found a secure spot near the latrine area. Now to wait for Lingo.

Elwin came and went—a temptation, but one he resisted. So did others, and the light was almost gone. He gave thanks for the nearly full moon. Finally, he saw Lingo come down. No one else was nearby. Walker gathered his courage, stood, and whispered, "Lingo! It's Walker, your old friend Walker. Over here. Come, please!"

Lingo looked startled and afraid, but enough words had come to recognize his old mentor. He glanced around, saw no one looking in his direction, then made his way toward the sound. Walker stepped forward and now whispered, "Thank you, old friend. I have news and a message."

Lingo clasped his hand and whispered, "It's terrible here."

Walker whispered, "Stay alive and hope. And give this message to Elwin of Adam's Family. Do you know him?" Lingo nodded. "Good. Tell him greetings from me, Walker, who has befriended Teller and his group. I will bring help in the spring. If you see my dog among you, I am here. (He motioned Dog to stand close and be seen.) My signal will be this bird song." He whistled a few notes, repeated them, and said "Repeat that." Lingo did.

"You must be absolutely sure not to be heard by a guard. Enough for now. Good cheer!" And Walker disappeared silently, leaving Lingo with his mouth open but a warmth in his eyes.

On the Monument's edge, two guards stood idly, casually watching the prisoners. They did not notice Walker.

"The fat woman is the nicest," said the first guard. "I think I'll give her an extra morsel tomorrow."

The second guard grunted. "Be careful. Strut doesn't like us making out with the prisoners."

"They don't practice what they preach. And what do they preach, anyway? Nonsense! 'The Sun God has killed the old one and made us his favorites.' What stuff!"

"More of that talk, my friend, and you'll never see summer again."

They chuckled together and went back to watching the women.

35

Northward struggled the eight in the first light of morning, their eyes to the ground for rooted plants and to the sky for rain. Ahead of them, the hills were drawing closer. Seven pairs of eyes scanned those hills for green vegetation, animal movement, and any sign of water.

It had been two more days. They had found that they could not walk effectively by night; the sky was clouding up and the darkness was absolute. So they walked morning and evening, stopping in the heat of midday, covering themselves with their cloaks against the sun, eating little and only plants, hoping for a little moisture for parched lips.

In the center of the group, Wing and Stride argued again over their course. "We can still turn east," muttered Wing. "There are bound to be streams running north to south, away from the hills."

"If we had followed the river, we would be walking east now, at the base of those hills," replied Stride. "Yes, there'll be water coming down from those hills; we'll find it. If only it would rain!"

"What if the river didn't turn east? What if it just kept on to the north?"

Stride was silent. Teller said, "Let's stop and rest for a few minutes. I want to look at you all." Slowly, they gathered, shaded on the west side of an outcropping. Teller studied each of them. To Tara, he said, "How is it with you?"

Tara said, "I am dry, dry. So are you. I can continue." She lay back and closed her eyes.

"What do you see to the north?" asked Teller, including all of them in his glance.

Kelso answered first. "There may be a little green to the east of north, may be a steep valley between the hills that would welcome a stream. No glint of water, but…"

Ayo said, "I see some darkness back in the hills. And there's a strong wind from the south. Rain may come soon."

"Stride?" asked Teller. Stride nodded. "Sure, we should alter our course to reach that point. How much longer? About a day. Would that we had a moon tonight."

"Wing?"

Wing grinned. "I could drink rabbit's blood. Let's do as Stride says."

Teller said, "Ayo, start a song for us." Ayo thought, then softly through her dry lips came a lilting melody suited for a quickened pulse and a hopeful march.

"Sun at morning, Moon at night, bathe us in your healing light."

Binta took up the song,

"Moon at even, Sun at dawn, light us till our fears are gone."

And they walked again, pacing themselves and staying together now.

Wing asked, "Does the Maker care about us now that we are exiles? Does he hear us talk?"

Teller answered, "He said he did."

***

Walker walked at night. It seemed that Dog could see in the dark, and he stayed at Walker's side, guiding him from hazards. So it was that in the pre-dawn twilight, he had reached the hills. From his bowl, he gave Dog some water, and they both looked around with care.

"I think they could not have come this far east," he said to Dog, who answered by turning west and sniffing the air. "They'll be dry and seeking the river, or any river… if we continue to the stream splashing down out of that canyon, and turn west, and watch for spoor… come on, Dog!"

As they walked on, a faint smell of smoke came upon the north wind.

Dawn came with no sun. Heavy clouds covered the sky, and the wind had swung to the southeast and was gusting. They were in the broad bottom of the canyon, all peering up at its walls, but could see little in the gloom.

"It's got to be raining up there," said Teller.

"Please, please," whispered Tara.

Stride held up a hand. "Listen," he said. "Do you hear that?"

It was as if the rustle of the wind were just a little louder. Slowly, it became deeper. It now resembled a faint roar. They looked at one another in perplexity, fear, and hope.

Teller cried, "It's a flood! Up the slope, quickly now!"

They scrambled up the eastern slope, rocky and now with trees. The roar increased. A wall of water raced down the canyon, sweeping all before it, rocks and tree limbs. It swept past them not thirty feet below. It began to rain. They raised their mouths to the drops.

A new voice cried, "Higher still, come up!" The figure of Walker appeared above them. "You'll be safe a little higher. You'll be safe now. Hurry!"

36

It had been an unforgettable twenty-four hours for the eight. From the grim sameness of the trek, they had spun nearly to sudden catastrophe and still more sudden redemption. There was thirst finally slaked, cold water rejoiced in, reunion with Walker, hunger satisfied, and sleep as deep as death, instead of death.

Walker waited patiently until the sun rose on a cool, beautiful north-wind morning to tell them about his travels. When he had finished, they interrupted one another with questions. How did Elwin look? And the others—did you see any of them? Would they survive until the spring? What were they building? Why?

Walker sat comfortably and pondered how to tell it all. "Yes, I think they will survive. There's a good deal more work to be done on the monument by the look of it. Their captors need them, so they will feed them. And knowing that we—that all of us—know where they are and have made contact will comfort them and give them something to hope for."

Teller asked, "How can we few rescue them? What are your thoughts?

"They are ill-formed, Teller, but hopeful. You are traveling in the hope of reaching a family that has stayed near the garden of the old stories. You hope further that they will confirm those stories, add to them, and approve your thoughts and desires. They will admire and trust you. If they do, perhaps they will be willing allies in a rescue effort."

Teller smiled. “That’s a lot to say. You know, not many suns ago, you were a feared stranger. Now, you are a rescuer and a friend. Will you come with us, help us to find the old ones?”

Walker smiled back. “I will if all of you will have me. During this summer, I have begun to feel that my life has surprised me with a purpose.” He looked around at the group. “Will you accept me as your companion?”

There was a jabber of voices saying, “Oh yes!”

“You will strengthen our purpose and our prospects,” Teller declared. “Tell us, how much have you traveled the way to the mountains and the Garden? Can you be our guide?”

“I have walked that way. There’s a large body of water several days ahead. You have to come just to the north of it. And a small river pours from the western end of that lake and runs west-southwest to join—or become—the Great River. You turned northward along the banks of the other tributary and missed that one. Then you will come to the foothills of the mountains. The garden is up on the western slope of those mountains. I haven’t been there, but someone long ago told me the way, and I hope I can remember it well enough to guide you. Whether there are men along the way and whether they are friends or enemies, I cannot tell. I have also heard tales of dangerous creatures in those rocks—non-human presences, heard but not seen, and feared.”

Stride said, “Speaking of beasts, we’ve encountered very few since the herd of antelope at the river. I thought this country would be full of life. Why isn’t it?”

Walker replied, “Well, it’s been dry this year, and the herds have drifted eastward to find good grass. Their predators have followed them. Have you enough food?”

Binta said, “Not for the journey you’ve described. And we need a few days here to repair our robes and water skins and get ready for cold weather. And to rest and heal.”

***

For the next several days, the group, now nine strong, made and mended. There were plenty of vines for rope, and enough plants to refurbish food and even medicine. Walker and Kelso fished until the rain-driven torrent dried to a trickle and did catch some good fish for drying.

Stride and Wing went upstream in search of animal food. They were gone overnight and returned late the second day with their woven bags full of trapped rabbits, skinned and the meat trimmed and packed in bundles of leaves. The girls foraged for good leaves, berries, and roots, gathered firewood (some to take to start night fires). Aaron helped with that, full of speed and energy. They were a very small army but a well-organized one, and by the seventh evening were packed and ready to travel.

Ayo sang to herself as she gathered and sorted. Wing was listening; the song made him smile and rock back and forth in rhythm. "How do you make such good songs?" he asked.

Ayo thought about it. "It starts with an impulse, then the words," she mused. "I know what I want to say in my song. Then I say it and change it, and say it again. If the words make a sort of rhythm, the song will come. I sleep on it and say it again the next day. And that's when the music comes into my head."

Walker was stitching skins together to make an all-purpose robe. Ayo and Kelso stopped and crouched to watch his expert hands make the stitches with a bone needle and plant twine. Ayo asked, "Walker, how do you survive all alone? With no one to help you hunt or protect yourself? It must be very hard."

Walker stopped to rest and sat back. He said, "It was hardest at first." A faraway look came into his eyes. "Staying safe, fire, weather, hunting, medicine, leather for robes, footwear, shelter… when I left my family, I knew only what a young boy knows. But the Maker kept me from killing myself for the first year or two. And I left with a gift—a knife made with a hard, dull orange-gray substance, priceless for a thousand tasks. I've learned from my errors and learned from men and women whom I met and made friends with.

"The most important things are water, fire, and food. Thirst will kill you the quickest. So I stay near streams or lakes in the hot summer and never venture out on the dry plains then. And people have taught me how to make water-tight bags and bladders.

"Fire, then. Cold is a terrible enemy in winter, and fire keeps him at bay. And it makes food better and frightens away animals. I lived without it, in fear, until an old man I helped gave me the second precious thing—this piece of rough, hard rock." He pulled a flint from his bag. "If I strike it with my flint knife like so—sparks come flying out, and I've long since learned how to scrape wood into fine feathery stuff that burns. I can start a fire in a hard rain now, under my body.

"Protection was luck and lessons. At first I ran from the big beasts, and slowly learned how to avoid them, detect their presence from signs in the ground or trees, how to use trees for safety. And then my knife helped sometimes to run them off. The worst enemy, as you know, can be men if they are greedy or selfish. So I'm very careful not to get surrounded—and I can run faster and farther than most of them.

"Sometimes I felt danger even when no one was near. I was being looked at by eyes I could not see, whispered to in nonsense words. I've had dreams like that, but these were no dreams. Dog felt it, too. My defense was to slip away as fast and far as I could go.

"Oh, yes, my third great precious find was Dog."

"How did it happen?" Ayo asked.

Walker smiled. "I went down toward the river at a place where antelope used to go for water. It was dawn. As I approached, I heard animal cries and the roar of a large cat; I became frightened and found a good tree to hide in. The cries subsided, but I waited in the tree for a long time till I supposed the cat would have gone off into the forest to sleep. Then, I crept down to the scene.

"There were no antelope carcasses, but there were the remains of two large … dogs. One family I knew called them wolves, but I have seen three different kinds in the world, and these were a little smaller and less hairy. They were dead and partly eaten. When I went up to them, I heard a small cry and found an infant dog lying beneath his dead mother's body. The cats hadn't bothered with him, he was so small. I took him and fed him as best I could, and he lived, and now we are inseparable. I play with him and give him treats, and he guides and protects me better than many fighting men. I owe my life and my happiness to Dog."

Dog heard his name and thumped his tail.

That last night, around the fire's now-welcome warmth, Teller and Walker reminisced while the others listened and drank water heated in wooden bowls with an aromatic spicy plant they'd found. (Teller's brandy supply was long gone.) A new moon was in the western sky.

"How often have you passed this way?" Teller asked. "Twice," said Walker, stretching out his arms comfortably. The first time, oh, thirty years ago or more, I was just a lad. It was late winter and colder then. There were hairy deer and wolves, and I didn't have Dog here to keep guard for me. I slept scared and kept a fire going all night if I could and slept in the morning.

"Did you see any other men?"

"One morning, at first light, I thought I did. A single creature, man or woman I know not, staring at me among the trees. A hundred feet away. He, I'll guess, was shorter and hairier than I, with a short cloak and a long walking stick. I couldn't see his expression, and he did not reply when I called to him. I had my sharp stick ready, I'll tell you. But after standing there still as a stump for a long minute, he just vanished into the woods. After a while, I went over there to look at his footprints, but the ground was dry, and there was no trace of him. It was a strange feeling to look at him. A man but not the same kind of man, it felt like."

Teller nodded. "When I was a boy, we saw some such creatures in the hills west of here. My father thought they were a man and a woman but without a child. Pretty far above us. He shook his spear at us and they disappeared, just like you described. Father said they were 'the old ones.' I asked if they were one of our families, and he said no. That was at night. The next morning, we went up to look. There was a hollow in the rock with a few bones, and on the wall, someone had drawn curved lines with a piece of charcoal. I thought they were beautiful. I still remember what they looked like."

"So there are other creatures like us, but not us," said Wing, entranced.

"There were. They're in the story, you know – a part you haven't memorized yet. Long ago – halfway in time back to the father, hundreds of summers, when the ice was here."

"What happened?"

"It was autumn, and our ancestors (whom I'll call 'we' and 'us' for the story) were foraging between the river and the hills, trying to find extra food and hides for a cold winter. We came across the scent and signs of an antelope herd, just what we wanted. We rested and drank and sharpened our stone spears. And next dawn, we started on the trail, up a valley to the north. It was cold already, but no rain or snow. At midday, we found the antelope, watering at a lake where the valley closed above them.

"As we prepared to take the antelope, we saw them – the Old Ones, a band our size with weapons, descending stealthily from above the lake. They saw us, too. And the antelope saw both. And all of them saw, creeping out from the forest, the pale yellow figure of a huge cat. It stopped. And for ten long breaths, nobody moved or made a sound."

Everyone was listening, captivated.

"Then everything happened at once. The Old Ones started screaming and waving their spears. Our hunters did much the same and began to run up the valley toward the antelope. And the animals, startled and confused, actually broke into two bunches, half trying to race down past us, the others up the hill where the Old Ones attacked them. Each group killed several, enough for our needs, and the rest vanished up or down the slope. And the two groups stood facing one another, as far away as that tree, smiling and waving their hands in the air.

The cat was gone. Whether it had left with dinner, no one knew.

"Good hunting!" our leader yelled. One of them yelled back, something we couldn't understand. Our leader advanced, holding his spear sideways in both hands. The Old One did the same. They exchanged spears, touched shoulders, and returned to their groups. In fact, both groups slept in that valley that night before packing up and departing the next morning.

"Did we ever meet them again?" Tara asked.

"No, there's nothing more about them in the record," said Teller. "I think the Maker knows them, and they just have a different story than ours."

***

The next morning, they set out, with energy and optimism renewed.

37

Fifteen days of glorious crisp fall weather went by, and nine humans and a dog stood on the eastern shore of a vast cold lake (which they decided to call "East Lake") with their backs to the intense yellow-orange light of the setting sun. Days earlier, that river Walker had described appeared in the distance to the south and came closer until they were on its north bank when they reached the Lake. The Lake's north shore had been flat and quiet, except for an inlet with a cave in its depth, looking dark and unfriendly, which they had passed with relief.

They stared across the plains at the mountain. The main peak rose out of a vast expanse of plain and foothills, distant but huge, a perfect pyramid whose upper, steeper slopes were already white with snow. A much smaller peak lay to its right, south of the giant and southeast of the travelers. At the west end of the lake, there were *two* rivers flowing out, one to the west (their river!) and one to the south.

Despite the cool air and golden sunlight, the mood of the group was sober and flat. On the trip down the lake's north shore, it had been relaxed and congenial, but now there was more silence than laughter, just a feeling of vague unease.

Walker had fallen in easily with the eight, taking his turn at hunt and watch. Every dawn, when Teller and Stride planned the day's trek, Walker was there to give guidance based on his experience. Near the lake, plants and game had been plentiful, and a couple of animals taken had furnished, after much scraping and chewing, leather for enough cloaks. Ayo modeled one, which was secured with a vine belt. Stride observed it with approval, remarking that the cloak would repel tigers—except for the human sort.

Now they were looking at ground none had traveled, and Walker struggled to reconcile the sight before them with the directions he'd heard more than twenty years ago.

"The sun will rise tomorrow over those mountains," he said. "We must be awake and looking carefully. On the morning of Equal-Day-And-Night, that sunrise would have been south of the peak and three sun-breadths south of the ascent we must aim for. That morning was, what—twenty days ago?"

Teller nodded, moving his hand in a "sort of" gesture.

"And the sun moves south in this season," Walker continued. "So, sunrise tomorrow, it will be south of the peak by, say, seven sun-breadths. We'll adjust by so much and take our course from that."

"How long a trek then?" Wing asked, glancing at Tara.

"Oh, six days to reach the foothills, ten more climbing," said Walker. "Maybe longer; I think the weather won't be good. There was talk of a stream for part of the way and crevices to shelter in. But it's climbing, hard climbing."

"I'll build the fire," said Binta. "We need to eat well and sleep warm tonight."

She and Wing set out to find fuel.

Later, sitting around the embers, Stride asked the big question. "How will we know when we are there?"

Teller smiled. "I've been thinking about that all summer, Stride. What was the place like twenty lifetimes ago? Is there still a family here, still guarding the places and keeping the memories alive? I hope and believe there will be. We'll just have to climb and watch and cast about and look for signs. It will be high up, near the snow."

"We've seen signs here, on the shore, the past few days," Stride said. "Ashes. Stones rearranged. Some scrape marks as though something was dragged to the water. People have been here."

"May they be friends," said Teller. And the group prepared to sleep, wrapping themselves in their deerskin robes.

***

In the late hours before dawn, the wind grew cold and snappish, and muted howls could be heard from away to the south. The searchers awoke restless, settled down again, and dreamed.

Tara dreamed she was alone on a mountain slope, with the smell of slavering wolves in the wind coming down from above and no shelter in the rocks below. She called out to Priam to come, but his answering voice was so weak, so far away. She crouched in fear and awoke shivering.

Wing found himself back at his family's camp before the trouble, trying to remember a sequence from the oral history. His ancestor had said something very surprising and important, but the words just wouldn't come. He mouthed, "and we fought off, we fought off..." but he couldn't say what. Then he remembered what it was, but he was afraid to say it. He awoke in a panic.

Ayo's dream was similar. She was making up a new song, and a word she didn't know, Aima, kept slipping in. She tried the line again, and it was Daima, then Daimo, then Deimos, and each time, the song became colder and more tuneless. She woke with a feeling of futility.

Binta was sitting opposite someone in a robe and cape, invisible. She said, "What shall I do?" The other person just kept saying, "No, no, don't trust them, don't trust them," in a soft, breathless voice. She tried to walk away, but it was too dark. The voice said, "Look what they've done. Stay with me."

In Walker's dream, Dog was gone, and he needed to go back and find him near the flooded place. No one listened to him, and Dog didn't answer his call. "What shall I do now?" He said to himself. No one else was looking at him.

Kelso dreamed he was lonely but didn't know for whom. He kept looking around but didn't see anyone. He saw a beautiful girl's face from long ago and turned west to find her. The face vanished, and a new, ugly face took its place.

Stride didn't dream, but his sleep was restless, and he awoke afraid, wondering whether something was wrong.

Teller was in a clearing, with trees all around him and bright sunlight. Whoever was talking was behind him and could not be seen. He couldn't bring himself to turn around. The voice asked, "What if the stone denies all you think you know?" He answered, "That can't be." The voice chuckled. "They made all that up about the Maker. There's no such person. I was there." The voice was penetrating and smirking. That's all he remembered.

***

The next morning, there was no sunrise, just black replaced with gray. Solid clouds covered the eastern skies. No peaks were visible. The wind, heavy and damp, was from the northeast.

It was a silent group that ate and prepared to travel. But no one spoke of dreams until Teller himself said, "Last night, some thing or person spoke to me in a dream. The voice warned me to give up hope in our quest. Did anyone else have a dream like that?"

All looked at Teller with amazement. Tara and Binta raised their hands simultaneously. Slowly, the others followed. Each one told of what they remembered and of the fog of fear and confusion in which they'd awakened.

Then Teller said, "Clearly, we've been discovered and attacked. Someone wants us to give up our quest. I find that very hopeful!

There was no discussion but a pulling together. The feeling now was strong of being a team facing danger, trusting one another. They broke camp with sober purpose.

Walker and Stride had been especially careful to map out in their heads the approaches to the likely route. They conferred and pointed. Then they all set out, not fast, leaning against the air. Stride kept looking back and forward and adjusting their direction. The ground, sparsely covered with grasses, sloped gently upward.

It took three days, all cloud and wind, to reach the actual foothills. The wind shifted north the second night and grew colder, but the morning was clear, and the sun showed its top right up a valley. They adjusted course to the right, still a little north of east, and found another valley, wider and steeper, going northeast. Encouraged, they adjusted cloaks and straps and sandals and began to climb.

38

Now, on both sides, there were lots of trees, tall ones with slender trunks, some with needles, and some with jagged-edged leaves. The right side of the valley flattened and became less definite, and then another valley split off to the right and downward. In front of them appeared a stream, narrow and gurgling, bright with fast-moving water. The stream fell off to the right into the new valley. Staring into it, Stride and Teller saw small fish, gray with hints of rainbow colors in the sun, flashing down and away.

They stopped to eat a little and drink. The water was finger-numbing cold. They gazed up the river valley and its green walls as far as they could see, which was not very far, but still saw no signs of humans. Looking back to the west-southwest they could see on the plain the lake, looking small, gleaming in the distance. Everyone looked around and gathered whatever wood they could carry; a fire would feel good this night.

Far above, there was a movement on the slope, but no one noticed.

The days were getting shorter; the sun was lower in the sky. The valley turned a little northward as they climbed. The evening sun disappeared over the western wall of the valley to their left; they could no longer see the plain or the lake.

Now, the stone sides of the valley drew closer to the stream. The ground was rough; they walked in single file now, with Stride in front and Wing in the rear. The air was colder, but they were shielded from the worst of the wind. Their climb had long ceased to be a picnic; it was becoming an ordeal.

Finally, in dusk, Stride halted and the others caught up. "Here's a place on the left where we have room for a fire and shelter from the wind. What do you think?"

Teller spoke for all of them when he said, "It's fine. I'm ready for a rest."

They had to ford the stream to its northwestern bank (left, if you're looking upstream), but it had widened and shallowed here and presented no problem. Soon, Walker had a fire going, and everyone was relieved and as comfortable as aching legs allowed. Food was simple, mostly just meat warmed on sticks. Ease and warmth gave birth to a little chatter.

"Well, your fat friend is glad of even a rocky bed tonight," ventured Tara between bites of an onion. "I could sleep standing up."

"Not much fat on you, Tara. Just a pleasing shape. And you're as good a climber as any of us."

There was a general chuckle; only a straight boy like Stride could get away with that.

"I think we're halfway up," Teller observed. "What do you think, Walker?"

"Hmm, maybe. There's more and colder climbing before we start seriously looking about for people."

They had gathered close together against the concave rock wall, with the fire in front of them and the stream just beyond. It was black dark now, except for the quarter-moon overhead and the embers, and night noises had gone silent. One by one but quickly, all the travelers were down, beneath their robes, with packs as pillows, sleeping.

A very low growl came from the river, answered to the left and right of them across the dark, warm embers. A louder growl-howl, scurrying noise, and a wolf was in amongst them. They awoke in momentary confusion, and then Stride yelled in pain as the wolf's jaws found his thigh. "Wolves, wolves! Attack, attack!"

The others were all on their feet now, grabbing in the dark for staffs and stones. More wolves were closing on them; the noise was chaotic. Then the greatest noise of all, a great barking, was heard as Dog leaped into the group and hunkered before the wolf leader, moaning and slavering.

Humans and wolves froze in position. The only sounds were those made by the two animals. The young men grasped their weapons and searched in the dark for the just-visible gray shapes. Four, five wolves?

Dog straightened up and made another terrible howl. The lead wolf backed up in small jerky steps, stopped, turned, and disappeared. His pack followed.

Binta found scraps and started to coax the fire back to life. Teller called out, "Answer each as I call your name, and are you injured?"

"Stride!"

"Here, bitten on my leg, can't get up."

"Wing!"

"Here, no."

"Binta!"

"Here, no. Making fire."

"Wing!"

"Here, arm and face scratched, not bad!"

"Tara!"

"Here, no. I'll see to Stride now."

"Walker! Here, no. Neither is Dog."

"Ayo!"

"Here, no."

"Kelso!"

"Here, no. Watching at the river, no signs of them."

"Aaron! Here, no."

"Nor am I hurt," Teller said loudly.

Stride's thigh was bitten deeply, and he had bled quite a bit. But the bleeding was down to a trickle, and Binta managed to get it stopped and the leg wrapped with a piece of leather, leaves and vine. Wing's injuries were shallow, dressed with a poultice from Binta's medicine bag. They set a watch—Elwin and Ayo to start with—and sat around the remnant fire.

"We can't leave Stride, and I don't want to split up," said Teller.

Walker said, "It might be good to send one or two of us ahead, try to make contact with the people who dwell here. We've seen their signs all up this canyon."

Teller thought. "We've got to have enough strength here to keep the wolves off. You and Dog are essential, and so are Wing and Kelso. I should go alone."

Binta spoke up. "I should come with you for extra eyes and a little protection. The others can get along without me."

Teller asked, "Who would keep a fire going?"

Walker said, "I will. I would very much like to accompany you, Teller, but your reasoning is sound. Let's rest. You'll need daylight to travel safely."

Soon, they were quiet again, but no one slept much.

As soon as they could see in the morning, Teller and Binta ate bread, shouldered their packs, and started up the mountain. It was cloudy again, windy and cold. They stayed on the left side of the stream until the path became too narrow, then forded across, and repeated that maneuver two more times. Another small stream joined this one from the right.

"What should we be looking for?" said Binta after a while. "You know, clues to where they're living."

"Just anything," Teller replied. "I've been hoping that the canyon would end by flattening out into a meadow and there would be the garden. But that's just a hope. Maybe even a dream." He smiled. "Dreams do carry the truth, sometimes."

"Yes," Binta mused. "And other creatures may, too. Sometimes I hear sounds or see a flash of motion in the distance and feel that some fairy creature is going by, sharing this world but unconscious of us."

"There are many such stories and strong beliefs. Other races, not human, kind or cruel. Before I die, I'd like to meet them."

And indeed, both of them were quick to look up or sideways after each little rustle or flash of a disturbed branch.

Teller set as good a pace as they could keep up, but by late afternoon, they were struggling. Then it began to rain. The rain was worse than snow; it dripped in under their cloaks, intensely cold. It turned to sleet, and the footing became treacherous. Slower and slower, they climbed. The canyon turned to their left, north-eastward, trapping them on the opposite side between river and rock. They inched along. The sleet turned to snow. It was getting dark.

The canyon wall to their left twisted right in front of them, to the water's edge. Teller sagged against the ragged rock face and said, "We have to stop."

Binta shook her head. "We have to find a better place."

Teller said, "I'm tired."

They became aware of a whisper of warm air to their left and a dim yellow light on their cheeks. A voice said, "Strangers, welcome. We've been expecting you. My name is Rememberer."

39

It was the next evening. The rest of the travelers had been found by their hosts and brought up to warmth and safety. Stride had two helpers, each arm over one's shoulders, to keep weight off his bitten thigh. All of them now sat in the cave, shivers disappearing in the fire's warmth, each with a stone bowl containing a wonderful warm drink. Their wet clothing was drying against a far wall, and dry cloaks had been provided. Rememberer said, "You can sleep here. We will become better acquainted in the morning."

***

Morning came clear and cold, with new snow covering the rocks. The travelers were given water and food, then sat to attention in their circle around the now-replenished fire to listen to their host. Looking around them, they saw a large, low-roofed cave with three tunnels leading away into darkness. The central open area was lit by high openings in the rock, and the air was fresh—one of the tunnels must be open to the outside on its far end. The walls were smooth, and supplies were neatly stored against them in bags and wooden boxes. A dozen human faces peered at them from around the tunnel entrances, most with welcoming, curious smiles.

Rememberer rose and stood in front of their semicircle. He was a small, well-padded white-haired man with a rounded face and features and a pleasant tenor voice.

"We've been keeping an eye on you since you turned up at the lake," he said. "You seemed peaceful enough, but we had no idea what your intentions were, so we just watched. Then you started up the valley straight towards us. We would have confronted you tomorrow.

"My name is Rememberer; my young relatives call me 'Memo.' You may call me that, too; it saves time. I will tell you more about us soon, but first, we would like to hear your story."

Teller, in his turn, rose. He was at one end of the semi-circle of travelers, on Memo's left.

"Sir, we all thank you for safety and shelter last night. We had been attacked by wolves. We were tired, cold, and beaten about, and one of our group was badly bitten. We were near the end of our strength. You trusted us and welcomed us, strangers, into your safe refuge. By this, you have made us your loyal friends."

Memo nodded his head. " Hospitality, not suspicion, is our way with strangers. Who would travel otherwise?"

Teller smiled. "That is the old, good way. Of late, we have seen other ways. Let me introduce to you all my fellow travelers. Next to me is Binta, then Walker, then Wing, then Stride (our strongest, but our injured man), then Tara, then Ayo, then Aaron and finally Kelso." Each bowed in turn.

"I will tell you about us and our travels in detail, but first hear our purpose. We are here on two quests. Our first was, and is, a search for the garden, the land where the Maker spoke to our first father and mother and taught us speech and purpose. Our history, which I keep in memory, tells that we are direct descendants of them. And I have inherited and possess a stone on which my teacher believed were marks that could teach us how to put down our stories on stones, to keep them for our children's children. The stone is broken, a large fragment is missing, and we cannot tell what the marks are for. I shared this story with our young people, and they agreed that it was so important to learn what it says that we would try a great journey back to where the story says the garden might be and try, by chance or with the Maker's help, to find the other portion of the stone. And, if great good fortune befell us, to find people who have kept the story of the first humans and can correct our version of it. Five full moons have witnessed our walk from there to here."

Rememberer kept his silence, but he was leaning forward with a frown of intense concentration. Teller continued:

"Our second quest arose out of a tragedy which impelled us untimely on our way in fear of our lives. Our family was attacked by another whom we thought were fast friends—in fact, Binta (he gestured to her) was betrothed from that family to ours. We were preparing for departure on our quest, and had just enough warning to escape. Fleeing up the Great River we met Walker, a remarkable and trustworthy traveler. He gave us word that our family's people who were not killed had been enslaved in the South. They are being made to build a great monument to an unknown God. Walker helped Kelso, who escaped from that slave prison, to join us.

"So, our second quest is to travel southwest and find a way to help our family escape. In this quest, we will be asking for your help."

Rememberer said, "Your story is both troubling and very exciting. You have been guided well! I believe the Maker has been your guide. The garden is close, and I am the historian of the family which returned here after our parents' families broke apart to guard the place and its memories. We also stay in the hope to receive and remember tales from the humans who have scattered to far places if they send messengers back. We asked this when the breakup happened, and many came back in the early years. But few now. You are the first visitors in seven years and you did not know for certain that we were here. We sorrow with your sorrows. We'll speak more of them soon.

"But the story of your stone fills me with excitement and hope. Booker, come here, and bring it."

A young man, stocky like Rememberer, hurried to the front of the cave, carrying a large leather pouch. "Here it is, Memo."

Rememberer took the pouch and very carefully, extracted from it a stone, large and darkly gleaming and filled with chiseled marks. He held it up.

At this, Teller stood and, trembling with excitement, drew his stone from his bag. He approached Memo. Without a word, Memo placed his stone on the flat ground with the broken end to the right. Teller placed his down, broken end to broken end. They came together as one, the crack barely visible.

"Come and look!" Memo cried. Others from deep in the cave hurried up, knelt, and stared. The travelers stood looking over their shoulders. Booker said, "Look! There's another column. It all matches up!"

Memo rose and gestured them away. "This is a wonderful moment in our lives. But we must take care not to spoil it. Teller, three of our young ones have made a long study of our portion. May one or two of your travelers join us, while we now try to make sense of it?"

Teller looked at Wing, who was practically dancing with eagerness. "Wing, here, is my apprentice historian. He has memorized most of what I know, and together, we have scratched our heads over the stone. He will throw me down the mountain if I don't let him join your team." He looked left and right. "And Aaron, will you help them?"

Memo looked left and right. "Wing, please join Booker, and here are Eber, Karana, and Elanor. Take it to your workplace. Slowly! Teller, I appoint aim keepers of the stone."

Teller asked, "'Aim'? What do you mean?"

Memo laughed. "Oh, that's a word we use to speak of both men and women. 'Ai, he or she; 'Ais,' his or hers, 'Aim,' him or her. They save a little time."

The Language Team walked away solemnly, Booker and Wing carrying the two halves.

"Give them a few days," said Memo. "They'll report any progress to us. Meanwhile, my other young people will show you our cave and the places outside where we plant and harvest roots. Teller, let you and I take a walk."

Teller readily agreed, and the two older men walked to the cave entrance, Memo in the lead.

40

They climbed together up the rocky slope beside the river, until they came to a brisk stream that flowed into it from the right. They followed this stream with more difficulty because of its narrow bed, sometimes walking in the shallow water (briefly as it was ice cold.) After about half an hour, the stream bed broadened, and on their right appeared a roughly circular meadow, about a mile across, ringed with forested slopes. A tributary stream flowed across the meadow toward them.

They followed that stream to the center of the meadow, where it bubbled up in a fountain from the rocky ground. Trees lined the stream, forming a covered avenue from the forest into the meadow, ending in a circle around the fountain. They were almost bare of leaves, and the meadow grasses were brown and dry where not snow-covered, but still the effect was serene, as of a secret place. The great mountain loomed above, white with snow almost to the meadow's edge.

"This is the garden," said Memo.

They found stones to sit on in the shade of a varied group of trees and bushes near the fountain. They sat facing a slab of fine-grained, smooth rock, a sort of table. Memo looked at the table-stone and smiled.

"We have another stone, you know," he said.

"Oh?

"It's larger. It's not in columns. It's just completely covered with the shapes, line after line. There are many different ones, and they're repeated in an irregular way – no pattern we can discern, except that certain groups tend to repeat."

"Are the shapes on the first stone?" Teller asked.

"Most of them, yes. It's our tradition that what the Maker said to our parents is recorded on this stone. And we can't read it. It's so frustrating. That's why we were so glad to see the missing part. We hope it will somehow reveal our true and whole story."

"It's a worthy hope!" said Teller. Then he sat silent for a few moments, thinking how to say what he was going to say. Then he straightened up. "Memo," he said, "When we slept down on the eastern shore of the lake, strange dreams came to us —to all of us. The dreams told us to be afraid and made us afraid. We were told to go back, to get away. Is there something we should know?"

"Yes," Memo said. "That place, near the cave, is like that. It emanates gloom and fear. There are two other places like that on the mountain. Not near the garden, but elsewhere on this mountain. Plants are stunted, and animals avoid them.

Always a cave is there, dark and forbidding. It's a concentration of evil. We don't know the cause, but we think creatures may live in that cave, unseen."

Teller thought about that chilling information. Then he shook his head and said, "Well, tell me now something of what might be recorded on that stone—what your stories say about it, about how he taught our father and mother, and what happened."

Memo sighed. "It was very long ago. And, like you, we only know what the stories have passed down to us, mouth to ear. Here's what our Recital says happened.

"First, that the Maker came suddenly and told Adam and Eve, the father and mother, that they had disobeyed. After an abrupt separation from the Maker, they left the garden (going right down the mountain, the way we came up.) They traveled down towards the lake but stayed well south of it, in the forest. They had the knowledge the Maker's angels had taught them and the two stones, but no tools, just a few sticks and bones.

"The forest was alive with birds and game, and roots and seeds and fruits were plentiful. During the next few decades, they had their family—three children, Cain, Seth, and Elanor (a brother, Abel, died as a young man)—and their grandchildren, the children of all three, seven in all. And then the father and mother died. So, the family lived as nomads in the forest for a long time until the cold began to come. And when it came, bitterness came with it."

"Who were the spouses of the three children?" asked Teller.

"The Story does not say. They had to be cousins. The Tribe—now nearly a hundred strong—had grouped itself into three families, and their quarrels bubbled up. Over whose fault it was that the Maker spoke no more to them, or that the world was growing cold and the animals more vicious and the land less fruitful. Over what to do about it all. Remember—the Recital says nothing about why the Maker sent Father and Mother away, except that a promise was broken.

"Each family had its own guess at the answer and would listen to no other. Cain and his family blamed the Maker for betraying them, and decided to go east in search of warmth. Elanor and her family blamed Cain (and their father Adam) for making the Maker angry and departed to the South in search of new lands. Seth's family blamed the other families for making too much of their resentments and stayed in place when the others left.

"Another generation passed. Humans lived long in those days. Seth's family believed it was the heir to Adam and Eve. It split up again, but more peacefully, and its groups became families and went west and south, seeking warmth, adventure, and solitude. That was when twelve of them—the founders of our family—decided to stay behind.

"They did it with their comrades' blessing, and in the many lifetimes that have passed, some messengers from them have returned with greetings and stories of their adventures. And always with questions about the Maker—has He spoken? Has He returned? A hundred years ago a boy came to us from a family near the Inmost Sea. He said his family was moving north around the Sea to escape others who had forgotten the Maker. And he said they had a stone with markings. We asked that it be brought here. He agreed, left, and never returned."

Teller spoke eagerly. "Our fathers were part of Seth's family. We, too, believed we were his own family, the central one, and had the stone to prove it. We moved west, past one of the great rivers, seeking warmer, safer land." He shook his head. "How was the stone broken?"

"I don't know. Our stories don't tell us. Just that one family went off with the broken piece. We always asked about it when a messenger returned, but no one knew. Until you. It's wonderful to have it back." He stood up and stretched.

"If only it can teach us how to read it," said Teller. "And what we are forgetting. I wonder if there really is another one."

Memo said, "Yes, we are forgetting. Even the language is changing. Messengers who come back speak with new words. Like 'mere' for 'mother' or 'dee' for 'die. One man used 'Zus' for Maker. I asked him where that word came from. He shrugged and said the 'Priest' says it. 'Priest' seemed to be their word for Teller. As the words change, the history is corrupted. We are slowly becoming strangers."

Far northward, at the edge of the forest, an animal appeared in the distance. It was huge and hairy, with a long snout and thick tusks, and was covered with long, black hair. He turned his long face to them and stared.

"What is that?" asked Teller.

"We've only seen it a few times," Memo replied. "We didn't have a name for it, so we call it the Mammoth. It looks too big to exist!"

Teller smiled. "There's so much to discover."

Memo took a handful of berries from his pouch and gave half to Teller. He pulled out a wooden cup and filled it with cold water from the stream. They both drank.

"Now," he said, "Apart from the memories that I keep as Historian, there are stories that we hear, sometimes from strangers. I will tell you what they tell of the intercourse between our First Parents and the Maker. Their truth we do not know.

"The First Parents did not remember clearly the time when they were infants or children. Their clear memory seemed to start like waking from a dream when the Maker called to them."

Memo paused and looked away, then back. "They sat right here where we are sitting, Teller." He sighed. "I wish I could have been there."

"The Maker said, 'You will be the first of my earthly animals to have "Language"— to know sounds that stand clearly for things and actions. Using these sounds—we call them words—to describe these things, to understand them, and tell them apart one from another is called "thinking." You cannot think without words and ways to use them. So I have called upon other creatures from beyond this Earth, whom I call teachers, to make you masters of words and thinking. They will be with you for three summers.'

"The Parents obeyed, and during the first summer, the Teachers taught them words and sentences and numbers and how to use them to ask questions about this strange and terrible world. The teachers were called angels; they would come and go like shadows. And the Maker was to return and teach them more about their purpose.

"But somehow, when the Parents were becoming proud and strong in their new knowledge, and the Maker was about to declare them ready to explore the earth, something terrible happened.

"And abruptly they left the Garden, as I have told you. No reason why is in the stories. Perhaps the Parents were ashamed and never told their children. But there is this awful silence between us and the Maker, and we have only a fragment, a hint of what happened."

Teller said, "That is more than we knew." He rose to his feet, too, and stood facing Memo, hands on hips, looking down at his feet. Then he said,

"What does all this have to do with you now? With your family?

Memo smiled. "It was a long time ago. Here we are, together, in this wilderness, living from day to day." He gestured restlessly. "But living with a purpose."

"Go on," said Teller.

"We are keeping to the place where it all started—we humans, thinking, talking, learning, trying to understand love and hate—waiting, if you will, for more knowledge, and help, to be revealed. We can form some kind of bond between the men and women who have traveled apart into this endless earth. It gives us hope to believe that the Maker will return and His will for us will be revealed someday. I haven't said that very well."

"I see," said Teller. "Well, meanwhile, it seems you have a good life here in your cave."

"Yes. We're together. We don't travel far after our food anymore. We live in this cave and in surrounding places. We can keep things—tools, weapons, clothing, dried roots, and meat. We call this 'property' and have rules to govern keeping it and exchanging it. Having a cave is very useful and very complicated. The young ones want to couple with one another; we have rules of courtship and marriage and caring for the children. We have rules that say who is responsible for gathering and hunting, for cooking, for medicine—and for saying what the rules are."

Teller raised his eyebrows as he pondered the thought. He asked, "And where do the rules come from?"

"Well, the Teachers taught our Parents words for the things we must do and the things that are forbidden. Words like courage, love, truthfulness. And words for anger, greed, jealousy, revenge. But just the words. How to understand them and put them to use, we didn't know. But we found that we just *felt* that certain actions were good and others not. So we leaders have to turn those lessons and feelings into rules. Sometimes we just guess…"

"We, too," said Teller. "And some of it's easy to agree on—doing things for the good of our family, obeying our leaders. These things seem natural. Dealing with quarrels, with property, with strangers when we meet—that gets complicated, and causes arguments. I wonder whether our parents argued with the Maker?"

Memo roared with laughter. "He sounds hard to argue with! Let's go back to the cave."

41

Ayo had gone with a young Garden Family girl, Avis, to look at the mountain. They were watching as the sun grew lower in the west. The towering white mountain glowed pale gold, and a few birds sang in the trees.

Avis trilled a melody of several rhythmic notes. Ayo turned, surprised. "You sing! How fine!"

Avis blushed. "I like to sing. Some of my family do, too, better than I."

"Do you sing together?"

"Oh yes. We love to sing in chorus, and we have some old songs that all of us know."

"Sing me one, please," Ayo begged. Avis turned away for a moment, then sang out a profusion of notes.

"Let me try to sing it with you," said Ayo. Avis paused, beat her finger up and down six times, then started with a nod. Ayo started, too—three notes lower. They both finished the song fragment, then stopped and laughed.

"Oh dear, I started too low. I'll have to fix that!" cried Ayo. But Avis laughed and said, "Yes, but it sounded beautiful, some of those different sounds together, high and low. Maybe we could make that a new song."

They tried the harmony again and soon were able to repeat it. They walked back to join the others, good friends with a common love.

The young searchers were being shown around by their new friends. They stood near the cave entrance. Walker, Ayo, Tara, and Binta were there with Wolf, the Lleader of the Garden Family, and his young helpers Deik and Lac.

Walker asked, “How large is your family now, Wolf?”

Wolf said, “We've grown. We are about nine tens”—he held up his ten fingers—“in number, and we live well here.”

He looked around with satisfaction.

“Taking over this cave changed our lives, oh, six lifetimes ago. It's large, with extensions into the mountain. It's well-ventilated; light and air can come in above the entrance, and smoke from our fire can go out that way. There are two openings in the back tunnels, so we sometimes have a breeze.”

“From whom did you take it over?” asked Binta.

Wolf grinned. “From animals. Some large furry ones lived here, so the story goes. And they didn't want to leave. But one of them nourished our ancestors for a whole winter, and the others left.”

“Do you live here all the time? No more summer travels for food?” Walker asked.

“We send out hunting parties. Sometimes, they're gone for half a moon or more. But home for all of us is here.”

Lac broke in, “You can't believe how fine it is to be able to keep things, to keep winter things during summer, extra robes and bowls, everything—not to have to pack it all up when we leave.”

Deik added, “And we can take the time to make things here, in winter especially. To learn how to make our bone tools sharper, spearheads and better ways to fasten them, better stem ropes to hold things together—all kinds of tools.”

“Where do you eat and wash?” Tara asked.

Lac replied. “Well, our families scramble up and down the mountainside looking for food and things, so they carry some things to eat. But we have cooked meals together here at the cave fire whenever we can. We take turns cooking, roasting on sticks or hot stones or putting roots and leaves in bowls. We've found that clay bowls get hard and strong after they've been slowly heated—unless they break."

"Until they break," grinned Deik.

Wolf added, "We have the river to wash in and places away and below it to relieve ourselves and dispose of dirty things. It keeps the cave smelling good and keeps curious animals somewhere else.

"We sleep near the fire when it's very cold, but many of us have private places—back in the tunnels or even outside the cave, where we can sleep and keep our own robes and weapons. Some things belong to the person who made them or is given them, and some things are held in common, like food and some tools." He pointed to the cave walls. "We keep the common things in here."

Binta asked, "Where are the babies? And the medicines?"

Wolf said, "Oh, Bula takes care of that. Come on, I'll take you to her."

Ayo and Avis joined Binta to see the babies.

Bula, black-skinned and black-haired, plump and smiling, was in an alcove just inside the entrance to the larger side tunnel, holding a baby and talking to Tara, when the others arrived. Binta and Tara admired the little one, and Bula handed her to Tara to hold. Bula explained their routine:

"A new baby and his mother—her mother, this one—are kept here within sight and feel of the fire. Usually, we have three or four small ones and half a dozen mothers of older children who come by and help take care of the little ones and make food they can eat after they're finished nursing. They nurse for two summers, sometimes three. And we have them walking and outside by then to toughen them up."

Binta was impressed. So was Ayo. She and Avis had been rehearsing a new song; Avis said, "Bula, please, may we sing our lullaby to the baby?"

"Oh, yes," she said, and they sang.

"Bed warm.
Wind cold,
Sky full of eyes.
Moon round
No sound
Silent good-byes
All creatures ruh
Soon you will too."

Then another. In this one, the two sang lines four through six in harmony.

"Sweet baby, close your eye
I'll sing a lullaby
Sing you to sleep.
Sing to you sweet and low
Sing that I love you so.
Dream on oh babe of mine
Safe I'll you keep"

"That was beautiful," said Bula. "Please come any time and sing for them."

Binta then said, "Now, who takes care of the sick and hurt?"

"Mostly that same group of mothers," Bula answered. "But I'm the chief medicine woman, and I have my herbs and splints and ointments, my bandages, and pain relievers over here."

She turned to a facing alcove on the other side of the tunnel entrance.

"We call this the sick and hurt bay. And it is Memo himself who remembers the ways our fathers have learned for treating disease. The old motto is, 'To cure sometimes, to relieve often, to comfort always.' And we're always finding new herbs that help."

"What are your best pain relievers?"

"Well, there's a leaf that works pretty well, chewed, it makes your mouth numb. But truth to tell, it's the spirits—strong liquor made from wine. And that's a bit of a problem because if I keep spirits here, someone's always helping themselves when my back is turned. So Wolf's main spirits maker keeps his store well guarded."

Binta remembered Teller's little flask, shared after the rainstorm, and nodded.

***

Stride and Kelso were down the mountain with Thunder and Arrow, two of the Garden Family's hunters, learning how they did their jobs.

"Winter's a good time to hunt if it isn't too cold," explained Arrow. "The goats and deer and pigs get hungry eventually and come out. And they're sluggish."

"Which ones are the most dangerous?" Stride asked.

"Oh, the pigs. They mostly avoid humans. But you can't scare them, and they'll attack without warning if you flush them. It takes at least four of us, with spears, to go after a pig. Better have a knife, too." He showed Stride and Wing his weapons: hardwood handles with stone-sharpened bone blades. He had one he was especially proud of. It was a small wedge-shaped flint, just a perfect fit in his hand, ground at one end to a sharp edge. "It's always in my pocket—handy for a lot of things."

"And I carry this," said Thunder. He showed them his hammer, a thick shaft about as long as his forearm with a stone head. The stone was roughly spherical and had a hole bored through its center. It was attached to a matching depression in the handle with thick braided ropes, and one side was sharpened to a sort of dull blade. "I can crack a pig's skull with it—if he'll let me get close enough."

Stride picked up the hammer and marveled at its weight.

"I might could throw a stone that size," he said. "But a smaller one is better for me—faster."

He found one near the stream bed and demonstrated, hitting a tree branch twenty feet away.

Thunder whistled. "Nice. You can come on our next hunt. We go out in a team of ten, with food and rough shelter. We look for tracks and signs, usually for deer. Then we either try to flush them out or hide in trees where they come out for water."

Arrow added, "In seven days, we can usually bring in enough meat to last the family a month." He was quiet for a moment, then decided to ask. "Have you ever fought against other men? Enemies?"

Stride answered. "No. Our family was attacked. But we were away from the fight, and…."

He and Wing then told about the attack, their narrow escape, and their cross-country trek to find the garden.

"We know some of our family are alive, and we know where they are," Wing said. "We're going to go back and save them if we can. That will involve fighting, I guess. Have you done it? Fought against men?"

"No," said Arrow thoughtfully. "But maybe Wolf will let us come with you."

42

The next morning, Teller and Memo sat around the fire to hear the report of the Language Team. Several others joined them, including Wolf.

Booker spoke first for the team. "We think we have something. Eber, Karana, show them the stone."

The two placed the stone, carefully glued together with animal-gut paste, in front of the two elders.

"You can see that there are three columns. Two of them were on our part of the stone. The third is on the searchers' part."

"Explain, please," said Memo.

"The first column contains little drawings of simple things. Stick figures of the human body. Parts of the body—feet, knees, an eye. A bird, the sun."

"All right," nodded Memo. "Proceed."

"So. There are forty-eight different little drawings—we decided to call them 'Picts'—short for pictures—in the first column. Each item in the second column is a single, simple Shape—like a straight line up and down, or a circle, and so forth. There are only sixteen of them, so the second column next to the rest of the Picts is empty. There must be something that relates the Picts and the Shapes. But we haven't figured out what it is.

"Then you brought us the other part of the stone. I'll let Wing tell about that."

Wing was beaming and nervous all at once. He had a stick in his hands and used it to point to the top of the right-hand part of the stone, recently glued on. He said, "This part of the stone fits perfectly with the rest. It contains a third column with an entry beside each item in the first two columns. So there are forty-eight entries—one for each Pict in the first column.

Each row in the third column contains Shapes, exactly the same ones as in column two. There are Shapes in each row, all forty-eight rows. But not just one Shape in each row– three, four, or even five! We don't understand. All of us stared, and thought and talked about it for two days. We're still thinking."

Memo said, "Well, the Picts themselves make a kind of writing. A little picture of each thing."

"Yes, they do!" cried Booker. "You'd just need a very long list of Picts and know what they were pictures of. But we think there's more to it than that. Those groups of Shapes are different for each Pict. They've got to somehow tell something about the Pict they're next to."

Wing sighed. "We've got to keep working it out."

"Good job," said Teller, as he and Memo rose to their feet and clasped the hands of each member of the team. "I know you'll get to the bottom of it soon."

43

After the sunny lull, winter returned in full fierce strength to the mountain. Snow, wind and cold made travel a risk to life some days. Even going to the relief area seemed a risk to life to Stride as he fought his way up against the storm to the cave entrance. He entered wet and half frozen and flung his outer robe near others at the entrance, making his way to a place near the fire. He stretched out, arms high, luxuriating in the warmth.

Fortunately, there was plenty of firewood as the company gathered to talk about the searchers' captive families in the south and to make a plan to help them.

Walker gave the full story of his secret visit to the temple prison and his arrangement with Elwin by way of Lingo for exchanging messages.

"I think I can get current word about the strength of the captors and where they are when the time comes," he said.

"How many guards do you think there are?" asked Wolf.

"Twenty, twenty-five perhaps," said Walker. "Well-armed and brutal drivers of the work. But by now, a little careless about guard duty. They say, 'Where are the prisoners going to escape to?' And so they're less watchful. And, this is important, most of them don't love their work. They're basically slaves, too."

"Ah," said Teller, "they're driven by fear."

"And how many able fighters can Elwin gather from the prisoners?" Wolf continued.

"He will have been working, very cautiously, in that direction—never specific about plans, just whispering and judging. There are nearly a hundred prisoners, and half perhaps in condition to resist. No weapons, of course. And there's always a risk that someone will tell a captor what's up. Kelso, you were a prisoner there, do you agree?"

Kelso stroked his chin in thought. "Some will be cowards, loyal to their captors, maybe even believers in their gods. But at least half will follow Elwin. Twenty-five, maybe."

"So, we'll have your five, Teller," said Wolf, "and I think I can raise ten or twelve young fighters anxious to go. Plus Elwin and his twenty or twenty-five. That would be enough, if we can achieve two things: surprise and positioning. Please describe the camp in detail."

Walker spoke again. "At the center is the temple itself, a circle of perhaps fifty paces across, in a larger field about a hundred paces square. This is situated atop a broad flat-topped ridge with shallow sides, not a very tall ridge—twice the height of a man. The surrounding countryside is hilly, with rock outcroppings in fields of low scrub and grasses. A stream is about ten minutes' walk to the north; it flows westward into the Great River, about twelve hours' journey away.

"The temple has two circular outer walls, one inside the other with a passage between, made of bricks. They rise to the height of a man with his hands straight up. The space between them is seven feet, and it will be roofed. Inside the inner wall is a large open space to be floored with fine bricks. There is a large opening in both walls to the northeast. They bring the stones in that way. The main, public entrance will be on the south side.

"In the inner circle, the real temple, there are two sets of stones. First, six of them, standing vertically half again the height of a man, around the periphery of the circle with their backs embedded in the inner wall. The widest one is on the east side and will hold the opening where the sun's rays will come through at dawn on Equal-Day-Night Day. Second, two very large free-standing stones in the center, higher than a man, an arm's width apart. A horizontal stone will be placed atop these vertical stones to make a rough shape of a man with his arms outstretched. These are massive stones; I don't know how they could even move them.

"Abel, who can look like an inoffensive old man, has managed to be within hearing range of discussions. He says that on top of the horizontal stone will be an upright one with a circular hole ground out. The horizontal stone runs north-south, so the thin stone lies east-west, and the hole in it will shine upon a carefully placed smooth white stone on the wide western stone with a circle cut into it. The sunlight will shine inside the circle on Equal-Day-Night at dawn, twice a year. There will be room enough for many worshippers to see the light, and we suppose some special object for the beam of light to shine on.

"The rock outcroppings from which these stones are cut are about fifty paces northeast of the ridge. The prisoners' area is south of that, east of the ridge, with latrines east of their fire pit. Kelso?"

Kelso continued the narrative. "Their captors have their tents southeast of the temple, surrounding a fire pit, and their own latrines farther south. There's a large tent for the leaders. There's no water there, but their slaves bring it from the river. The tents are made of hides tied to tree branches, very nice looking, with images in some kind of paint on the hides. They plan to build a stone building for the priests after the temple is complete. Oh, and a small vertical stone-man, a miniature of the one in the temple, stands near the fire on a stone which raises it up."

Wolf nodded his understanding. "A very complete description; thank you. What it suggests to me is this. From the river, we move east along the stream, stop short of the ridge, and conceal ourselves there, north of the temple, the night before. We can scout the area from there without being seen. Then in pre-dawn darkness, half of us move south toward the tents, using cover from the ridge. The other half moves east along the stream and joins the prisoner-soldiers at the latrine. Just before sunup, the first group rushes the captors' tents, and the second group attacks the guards. Some of us will then move into the temple itself if there's anyone there. Does that sound feasible?"

There were a few moments of quiet consideration. Teller said, "It may be. So much depends on things we don't know yet. We'll need an advance party to contact Elwin again, find out his situation, his view. Stride, Walker, and Kelso could go."

Memo had been silent throughout the meeting. Now he spoke.

"Wolf, Teller—I have been listening to your words and thinking about your plan. It's courageous and warm-hearted to want to fight for these families who are being cruelly treated. But is it wise?"

Everyone went silent and stared ahead. Wolf said, "Go on."

"Our family is not threatened by this so-called Great Tribe. Here, we are strong and confident. Out there, we will be strangers with no knowledge and no allies. We are hunters, but we have never done battle with other men, thank the Maker. There is every chance that all of us could be killed or made slaves. I know I sound like a coward. But I think it needed to be said, and it needs to be thought about."

Teller leaned forward to address Memo, his voice warm. "You are right, Memo: It's dangerous and often evil to fight other men. You are our friends who saved us when we were in need. We will always be in your debt."

He turned to Wolf. "You have no obligation to help us in this risky plan to rescue our families. But we must go. A great wrong has been done, and only we can strive to set it right. And keep this in mind. Our enemy hates you too."

Wolf, too, looked at Memo with friendship. "Dear Rememberer. We will certainly think hard about your advice.

We may not go. Or we may go and attempt only a stealthy rescue of Teller and Elwin's families. We may return home without accomplishing anything. Or we may fight and die if we decide that our battle is just and victory probable. If we do, Teller, who will lead your men?"

"Stride; who will lead yours?"

"If we go, I will," said Wolf. "I welcome Stride at my side."

The meeting broke up then into a few smaller groups. Teller motioned to Tara and took her aside.

"You must not go with us," he said. "It will be the first moon of spring, and your child will be ready to be born."

She nodded and held his shoulders for a moment. He spoke again.

"I, too, will remain here. The others will return for us afterward."

44

It was Wolf's decision to make. Go and fight, or not? He had never made a decision like this before.

Most of his young people were enthusiastic for the fight, eager to save the captives. They could imagine the glory but not the death, he thought with a wry smile. They were told that an enemy of men had appeared and believed that if we, our family, did nothing, we'd eventually have to fight them. Was that true? They believed that to fight now, to help the good people who were prisoners, was the right, the noble thing to do. Was that right? The choice was the wisdom of holding back against the valor of fighting. The evil was true. So was the danger.

Perhaps it was true that a man had to wrestle with the Devil to be worth being called a man.

He had to think. To question the plan, to assess the probabilities, to hear the doubts, to remove the uncertainty. The certainty of decision would come nearer. But If you waited for perfect certainty, you'd be too late. A scouting expedition would be vital.

***

The talk in the cave was now all about the scouting expedition. Who to send, what route to take, what would be the meeting place with the main body, which must arrive in darkness when the day was as long as the night. Many of the young men and some of the women wanted to be in that main body.

Back in the quiet of the garden, Teller, Memo, Wolf, and Stride, along with Walker and Kelso, were making detailed plans.

"You've got to send us as a scouting party," Walker insisted. "Teller's right. Almost anything could have happened. Lingo could have been found out and killed. They could be waiting for us. They could have finished the monument and left or doubled their guard force."

"Yes, and the longer we wait, the more likely we are to be too late," Kelso added.

"Let's talk about time," said Wolf. "If you're going to go to the camp, scout, return, and brief us on the situation, then all of us repeat the journey, how long will all that take? Will it delay us too much? Should we just take a chance?"

Walker pondered. "Going around the lake will take time, especially if we get a lot of rain. Yet we want to follow that river that we now know of from the northwestern end of the lake to avoid striking straight across unfamiliar country. Do your hunters know the way around the north side of the lake?"

Wolf said, "Yes. I've spoken to our best ones. We knew that a river flows south from the southwest corner of the lake. But we also know that another river—the one you found—flows west from the lake at its northwest corner. It flows west-southwest along the foothills and then curves south to join—I think to become—the Great River."

"Yes," Walker said. "We thought we were following that river. But it turned north. That's when we left it and came east through the desert. We were amazed when another river appeared to our south."

Wolf lowered his head and pondered. "Walker, you were there. What do you think?"

Walker said, "I know what happened. During their flight, they joined the Great River and walked up what they thought was the main stream. But it was a tributary. The other tributary, the river that comes from the lake, was a little south of where they turned, and they didn't see it. When they did start east, that river was two days' journey south of them. We joined it finally west of the lake."

Wolf said, "So, if you take that river—it becomes the Great River—it'll take less than two days' journey from where you leave it to reach the temple, isn't that right?"

"Yes, it is," exclaimed Walker. "That makes it a shorter way to get there, do you see, Stride?"

Wolf said, "We've got a surprise for you. "Our hunters have a raft to float on the lake, with long paddles to move it. We can move the three of you across to the head of that northwest river in four days."

Walker rubbed his hands together. "That's good. Then we'll follow that river for about, oh, ten or eleven days. Then we'll leave it and strike southeast for the temple. I have not seen that part of the journey, but I estimate another two days."

Stride laughed and waved a fist. "That will save us time. Wolf, do you think you can take us down that river on the raft?"

"Hmm… I'm not sure it's wide enough all the way. It might be. But I don't like the idea of towing that raft back upstream for ten days."

"I know!" cried Stride. "Why don't we do it this way? We'll walk west and south along the river and then east to the temple. After our scouting, we'll retrace our steps and start back up the river. The main force can also walk west, but you can bring the raft downstream right with you, carrying food and weapons. That way, you'll go faster!"

"Excellent idea," Wolf said. "We can just leave the raft when we leave the river. Let's see: that's eleven days, plus two more going southeast to reach the temple. Less than half a moon.

"Our main body should meet the scouting party more than halfway back. We'll do it by leaving earlier than we planned."

Walker said, "Yes! We'll leave Eden seven days after the second full moon after the shortest day. We'll reach the temple before the next full moon, start our return just after it, and walk back for about seven days to meet you coming. Then we join and walk back to the temple, to reach the plain north of it at least two nights before Equal-Day-Night."

***

Wolf stared at the sky. "All right. What will the moon phase be when we get there?"

"Nearly first quarter. No moon the hour before sunrise."

Wolf mused. "It'll be hard going for you." Another pause, then, "You've met Thunder and Arrow of our hunting team. I want Arrow to go with you scouts. He's a fast traveler and could make a fast return if early news is needed."

"I'd like that!" said Walker. And the meeting broke up.

***

Memo had been silent for the entire session. Now, he gestured to Teller to stay behind.

"Friend," he said, "I want to agree with you on something important."

"Tell me," said Teller.

"Your young man, Wing, wants to take both stones with him on the rescue expedition. He believes you may go back to your home on the Great River, and finish the job there, and—I don't know what. I cannot agree to that. The stones should stay here, safe with us."

Teller sighed. "Well, we had to face these decisions soon, didn't we?

"The solution will be found by our families, together," said Memo. "Our history will be put on more stones and all the stones kept here safely where men from across the seas can come and read them. That's what I see."

"Yes, but this invention is too precious to stay in one place, to risk being lost if your family is lost," Teller said. "Both our families must start learning from the stones how to put down memories on stones or sheepskin—history, stories, songs, how we do things, everything—and never stop. And didn't you say the other day that a family out beyond the Inmost Sea may have a stone?"

"Yes," Memo said. "It may be just a rumor. It may be true."

"Let's both think hard about what to do."

45

In the cold, gray dawn of the second new moon since the days began to lengthen, the three men of Elwin's family left the cave and began their journey down the mountain. They were well-robed and capped against the cold, with leather sandals on their feet and a warm breakfast in their stomachs, and they carried on their backs tools and provisions for the trip. They would be met by Wolf's hunters and their boat at the lake. Dog was at Walker's side.

"I just keep thinking," Stride said, shivering, "that every day is going to be longer and warmer than the one before."

"May we find good dry leaves every night," Walker said, smiling, "And no long stretches without water, like four moons ago."

"And firewood enough," added Kelso.

"Well, we've pledged to reach the camp, confirm the plan, and return to the river fork by the next new moon," said Stride. "That's going to take some hustle. Oh, I hope they're all right."

Walker looked out to the west, where the glitter of sun on the lake water was just visible far ahead and below. He pursed his lips and narrowed his eyes thoughtfully but not grimly. "It just depends on the terrain... and the weather...and what the real distances are. And whether we avoid breaking our bones or getting run over by a pig in a hurry. We'll be fine!"

Stride laughed. "I'm all cheered up."

And down the path they went, two youngsters and one fit oldish traveler, happy to be on the march.

They reached the lake on the fifth morning. It was a big lake. They couldn't see the western end from where they stood. And waiting for them were three of the hunters: Hunter, Arrow, and Thunder, with a log-and-birch raft pulled up halfway out of the water behind them. Greetings were exchanged.

"The raft's ready," said Hunter. "We often carry three hunters and two deer, so it should fit us all nicely. Two of you forward, one in the middle with Arrow, all four of you to row. Thunder and me in the back, to steer." He motioned toward the rudder, a slender pole flattened at its end, held to a notch at the end of one tree. "We'll stop for a meal halfway through the day, change positions, and pull over at dusk for a fire and sleep. And we'll take shelter if storms blow up. We're taking Thunder along to help return the raft since Arrow is going with you. Walker, can the dog walk ashore or must he stay with you?"

"He can walk beside us ashore. We are inseparable; he'll know where I am." He looked with love at Dog, who bumped his leg affectionately.

Arrow added, "We've made this trip in four days, in perfect weather and winds behind us, and in twice that many in storms and snow. It just depends."

Kelso spoke for all three: "We'll row hard and sleep short. We want to reach our friends just as soon as we can."

Kelso and Arrow took the forward seats, climbing carefully the length of the raft. Hunter put the travelers' packs down the middle, and Walker and Stride took the second seats and were handed paddles. It was cold and cloudy, with a moderate east wind, a helping wind.

"Cast off!" cried Hunter, and the middle two paddlers pushed away, then the front two started rowing, Kelso carefully matching his stroke to Arrow's. The raft was a little wobbly, but it moved off at a decent pace. "Beats walking!" cried Stride.

***

They made good time, and as sunset approached, Hunter untersteered the raft leftward toward an inset in the shore where a tiny stream entered the lake. "We'll make camp there."

"How'd we do for speed?" Stride asked as they approached.

"Pretty good," said Arrow. "This is a good sleeping point we always use if we get here."

Thunder added, "You know, with the breeze behind us like it was, one of the men suggested we tie a skin between two poles and let the wind help us. But we haven't tried it yet. The wind is never directly behind, and I wouldn't know how to steer. And, of course, if it's blowing from in front, we'd just go slower."

"Good idea, though," pondered Walker.

***

They were off again the next morning after a cold meal and no fire, the work of rowing keeping them warm enough. The weather was holding, and the surface of the lake was smooth. Birds were plentiful. An occasional deer walked up to the shore for a drink, breaking the sunlit silence. All six men were strong, healthy, and untroubled, and the routine was set: a stop for food and rest, where the men changed places, then on westward. The forest was left behind, the shores now barren prairie, flat to the south, rising in the north to the foothills.

It was a little after noon on the fourth day that they reached the western end of the lake, along its northern bank. The hunters steered the boat over, jumped out, and pulled it up onto a sloped beach. They all got out and walked along the shore, here with scattered rocks, till they came to where the young river bubbled busily away to the west.

"What do you think?" asked Arrow.

Hunter scanned the stream's mouth, then peered down its length, slightly south of west, as far as he could see.

"I think the raft will slide down this river," he announced. "The river shouldn't get narrower—tributary streams will be entering it. Even if it hangs up somewhere, it will have saved us time. And I think we could use two for the main group and just leave them down south. It'll save us days."

Stride was counting on his fingers. "So, we estimate we'll reach the temple in ten, plus two, twelve days. If it takes us two days to make contact and agree on a plan of attack, we'll be back here in about twenty-two days. But if the main force can leave in, say, ten days, you'll meet us coming back up the river."

Hunter said, "What about this? We start as soon as possible, and you wait for us at the spot where we leave the river."

"Well, we don't want you too close too early—chance of discovery. How about you leave Eden eleven days after the new moon, sixteen days after we do? We'll meet about eleven days later and ten days from the temple. That'll get us to the Temple with just a day to spare."

"Let's eat a meal now," said Hunter. "Then we can start back; there's plenty of daylight left."

After a quick meal from the raft's supply of dried meat and flatbread, they turned the raft around, pounded shoulders, and the scout team started striding westward down the river bank at an easy pace, carrying their burdens. Hunter and Thunder watched them till they were out of sight, then climbed aboard the raft to row it, slow but sure, back east. With luck, they'd be met in a day or two by a couple of helpers.

46

In the cold, rainy night, the prisoners from Adam's Village huddled together under their ragged cloaks. They always slept together for warmth, safety, and support. The sleeping place was about fifty paces east of the temple gate, not walled in but guarded by two men who huddled together too against the drizzle, paid them scant attention.

All of Elwin's people, except the children, wore the scars of beatings, and all were thin from the careless rations they were given twice a day. But remarkably, no one was seriously ill. Now, it was three hours after sunset; the moon had not yet risen.

Elwin rose quietly, stepped away and headed for the latrine area. Art noticed, rose, and followed; it was their habit to keep together when they could. They relieved themselves and stood together, just looking around. There was a movement in the dark to their left, north, away from the latrine. No sound.

Art pointed. Elwin nodded, turned casually, looked around. The guards were asleep. Both men moved away very slowly and quietly. Twenty yards, then Elwin's thigh was brushed by Dog. He touched and followed a few yards more, and there were the advance guard: Walker, Stride, Kelso, and Arrow. Hands were clasped.

Walker had assumed leadership, and he whispered, "First, friends, tell us how you are and how many."

Elwin responded, "Oh, we are so glad to see you again. We are alive and ready. The work here is nearly finished, I think. Art and I have very carefully whispered to the others we decided to trust, and I believe no one has broken our trust. We have fifteen men and five women ready to fight."

"Excellent," whispered Walker. "We have twelve fighters armed and on the way. They'll be here in fourteen days. Can you hold out that long?"

"Yes, the Maker willing."

"Here's the plan we have devised," Stride said. "We will attack just before sunrise, with just enough light to see and get into position. We'll have one person, probably me, join you here half an hour before dawn, with one other as a messenger. We'll concentrate our men as close as we can without being seen to the leaders and other men near their building and wherever else you tell us. Your group on the signal, will attack and subdue the guards near you. Our two will join you right here before the signal and bring clubs and ropes to tie them with. Do you agree, and where else do we need to place ourselves?"

"Art," Elwin said, "where do you see the guards at that time?"

"The total number of people there'll be at their cabin is about nine: their chief, his woman, and his assistant, three who oversee the placement of the stones, and three guards. It's possible that three additional visitors may be here to witness the light beam, but they won't be fighters. The guards will be trained and armed with clubs; a couple of them have wooden knives as well, and there are spears in the leaders' tent. At that time, the chief and his lady will be sleeping, and so will two of the three builders (those four are normally unarmed). One of them will be in the temple planning the day's work. All six guards will be awake—three watching you prisoners, the others eating south of the Tent. It'll be a work day, so they'll be sober; on Rest Day, they would probably be full of drink and sleep."

"We'll assume they're alert," Stride said. "So, we'll have ten near the tent and two near the temple with you, Walker. I think we can leave the three guards to the prisoners and one of us; the others need to be as near the temple guards as possible, and three or four devoted to those in the cabin."

Walker said. "Let's make that three of us, one for each guard, with the prisoners, if Elwin agrees. And you're right; the rest should have specific assignments: the guards at their meal or the three watchers, the leaders in the cabin, and a group of maybe four to cover surprises. Elwin, I want to mark our people so that we know who's with us. What about having each one mark themselves with dark ashes on their foreheads? Are there ashes about and within reach?"

Elwin and Art turned to each other, nodding. Elwin said, "I think we can handle the three guards. Placing the others will be tricky. There's not much cover south of the cabin. Could your men creep in from the northwest, maybe using the west side of the temple for cover, and gather behind the cabin?"

"I think so," said Kelso. "We'll come down from the north in darkness."

And Art said, "There's plenty of ash around. I'll gather a handful and spread it as soon as we're awake. Your two can sneak over here to the latrine and be with us. Where will the signal come from?"

"From the cabin," said Kelso. "Wolf, our leader will be one of those there. And using Dog to alert us when you're ready would be good like you did tonight."

Walker said, "We'll leave you now. We're going to make a slow, careful trip to the south and west of the compound to see the tents and, in the distance, the temple entrance. Then we'll be away."

"Let me come with you," Art said. "I can show the way."

Walker nodded. "Thanks."

They whispered of other things for a few moments—of greetings and love to their companions—and then disappeared quietly into the morning twilight.

Elwin returned to the other prisoners. He laid down next to Gratia and whispered, "They came." Gratia squeezed both his hands. He turned toward the other Adam prisoners, touched a few shoulders, gestured "quiet." Slowly they sat up and gathered closely around their leader.

He looked around to be sure no others were within earshot, then spoke, in a hoarse whisper, "They came. Stride, Kelso, Walker, and a man from Eden, Arrow. We have a plan. The main body will be with us in fourteen nights—on equal-daylight day before dawn, twelve fighters plus our own. No words to anyone, even friends, now. Be happy, and gather your strength. Pray!"

They fell away and lay down again, feigning sleep, to wait until a guard kicked them awake. Elwin and Gratia lay together, her hand on his shoulder, her eyes closed. Art sat near Winnie. They heard a flutter above their heads and felt a breeze. The turtle dove dropped to the ground beside them and folded its wings. Its head rose, looking at their faces, and they saw that in its bill was a small green apple. Gratia held out her hand, and Gaby dropped the apple into it, stepped back a step, and gazed at them.

"You've come back!" she whispered. Elwin stared at the apple. He whispered, "Is the apple from Eden?"

Gaby nodded vigorously. "Do you know about the plan?" Another nod and Gaby brushed her with a wing. "Will God be with us?" A nod, a whistle, and away she flew, singing.

47

Five days before, in the darkness of the early morning of the full moon, Wolf had led twelve strong young fighters as they swung down the trail from Eden towards the lake. Of the searchers, there were Wing, young Aaron, and Binta, who had packed a full kit of dressings and herbs. The fighters from Eden included Deik, Lac, and Thunder. Teller and Tara stayed behind with Memo and the people of Eden; Tara was great with child.

The hunters had constructed a second raft so that all their team could ride quickly across the lake, food and weapons stored in packs beside them. It had been rainy and blustery for the last week, but it was warmer now, a sign of coming spring. Teller and Memo had watched the stars together and talked long talks, and they had found no hints of trouble to forbid the journey. A turtle dove had flown low over their assembly, circled singing, and headed high and west, somehow a spreader of energy and smiles.

"I wonder what we've forgotten to do," said Teller to Wolf. Teller and Memo were accompanying the team as far as the lake, coming along at their rear.

"Aye, there'll be something to plague us," Wolf replied. "I don't know who said it —plans are very, very important till you start, then you can forget them."

"We could have armed a larger group. We could have sought help from the village down south of us, along the Tigris. We could have tried to think of a plan to negotiate. But no time, no time." Teller shook his head. "I didn't think we'd be fighting this spring."

Wolf grunted. "Well, the object is not to have to fight next spring. Perhaps meanwhile, we can think of a better way to keep our villages friends instead of enemies.

"That's right. Let's try to learn from this one."

They parted at the rafts. The team, building on the speedy journey of Stride and his comrades, were going to try to get down the river in nine days, turn east, and hasten another day, then if they hadn't seen the scouts yet, hide and wait for the scout team to join and assure that all was ready.

Wolf bade Teller and Memo farewell, and Teller promised to have a backup team ready and a messenger down the river seven days behind them, just in case.

Wolf and Stride divided their men and women into two groups and loaded the rafts. Wolf was in charge, but he agreed that Stride's boat should lead the way because they'd just made the trip and knew the river. Off they went westward across the lake, now choppy with the spring wind, bouncing over the water as fast as energetic young rowers could propel them.

Maybe a little too fast. It was mid-afternoon, a good quick lunch having been taken ashore, and the rowers relieved, when the two men rowing on the right side of Stride's raft got their paddles tangled so that the energetic left-siders pulled the raft's prow to the left, a wave lifted it, and it went over, tumbling all eight of its crew into the water.

"Help us!" yelled Stride as the raft tumbled, tipping people and baggage down. Then, to his crew, "Swimmers, help the others, grab somebody!" realizing that he wasn't sure who could swim and who couldn't. "Yell for help!"

Stride, Wing, and two Eden hunters, Deik and Lac, could swim, and they each made sure to catch hold of another struggling crewmate. Wolf did his best to turn his raft towards Stride. As they closed, three swimmers jumped out, swam to the upside-down raft, and righted it. Swimmers closed on both boats in a flurry of splashes and shouts. Both boat leaders did head counts. Wing had hold of Binta; she was all right. All sixteen were pulled aboard, some coughing and retching, but all breathing. Then several of the swimmers dived back in in a belated scramble to save the bags full of food and supplies.

The lake wasn't very choppy at that point, but any packs still afloat were moving away. Hands grabbed for them and pulled them up. Two men dived down to see and save any sunken packs, but the river was too deep. Finally, everyone was back aboard, and a quick look around showed that most of the raft's baggage had been saved.

"Go ashore!" cried Hunter, pointing leftward to the nearer land. It was relatively flat, and both rafts were able to reach it and be pulled half-dry. Everyone got out and sat down, weary and recovering from the shock. Stride and Hunter counted their people again. Binta looked around and found her pack of medical supplies.

"Well, people, that was a good recovery from a dumb foul up," said Hunter. "I think we hurried too much before we were sure of ourselves. Now, don't blame yourselves or each other. There's no room for blame in this expedition. Just figure out how not to do it again. Stride, have we come far enough for today, or must we row west some more?"

Stride looked around at his people, and at the mess of wet packs on the ground.

"I think we've come far enough. Let's take care of our packs, set everything out to dry, and call it a day. An early start in the morning, and we'll get back where we should be."

"So be it." Hunter nodded, and the crew began to lay things out.

48

Three prisoners, Elwin, Gratia, and Abel, huddled together, talking in low voices. They were near others from their village family, but no one else was close enough to hear them. It was sunset on a day of gray and clouds, suddenly triumphing in a glorious sunset. The show was almost over, in darkness and stars.

"Let's call him 'God,'" said Elwin suddenly.

"Why?" said Gratia.

"Oh, the Maker is *The* God; it just feels more right to me."

"Does he want that?"

Abel smiled and interjected, "Good question, Gratia. I don't know. It might be too personal. Let's wait for a sign from him."

"All right," Elwin subsided. "You're right, Abel, you're the old, steady one."

"Old anyway," Abel chuckled.

Elwin yawned, "Well, the Maker seems pretty distant, but the Devil doesn't; he seems right in the middle of this camp."

"He does that," agreed Gratia. "Did you notice this morning? I was quite sure I saw Diss coming out of the leader's tent."

"No! Oh, that settles the question. They're all in it together!"

"I agree," Elwin said. "Diss is the Devil's servant, and his people were spreading their poison into our village wherever they could find a listening ear. I think they're still doing it, even in this prison. This is truly an enemy stronghold."

Elwin looked around, a finger to his lip, and gestured them closer. "Does that affect our escape plan? Are the other prisoners going to fight against us? Is the enemy too strong?"

"Let me think," Abel said. "Can we guess, from our conversations, how many of the prisoners are with them? Have we seen some get special treatment? Gratia?"

"Yes… there are always a few that smile up to the guards, that frown at us or move away. Among the women, I'd say eight or ten. But they won't fight."

"Some among the men, too," Abel said. "Friendly but… nosy, if you see what I mean. Poking in to see if we have plans. I'm glad they're still poking; it means they don't suspect. And I love playing the stupid, fearful old man. A few of the stronger ones have actually been recruited. They're either guards or were taken away. I'd say ten of the men would fight if they were organized."

"Okay," Elwin said. "But that's why our plan relies so much on surprise. Here's what I think we do. We've got enough volunteers to help Wolf take on the guards and still assign men to get close to the troublesome prisoners. Get close to them when we move out, quietly, waiting for the signal, and go after them if they start to fight. Assign specific men to individual suspects. Can we do that?"

"Yes, we can," said Abel.

49

In the pre-dawn moonless darkness, the battle party crept eastward toward the temple.

Elwin awoke to a cool sensation against his cheek. He sat up and looked around. Dog looked back, then sprang silently away.

It was the morning of the battle, and the war party from Eden was here. Quickly and quietly he stood up and began to touch his fellow Adam prisoners, one by one. Soon, he was surrounded by them: Gratia, Art, Abel, Maire and the rest. He looked around. The silhouette of a guard could be seen close by, black against the dark gray eastern sky. He whispered to the group. "To the latrines; tap our loyal prisoners, one by one; blacken your foreheads." They began to awaken their allies. No commotion yet. Good.

Stride and Abel appeared at his side. Stride whispered, "Good morning. Wolf's twelve are creeping up to the cabin; he'll give the signal when he can tell a black thread from a white. Any changes?"

"The leader has two visitors. They came yesterday from the southwest, a village on the Inmost Sea, I think. They walked all around the construction, judging progress, measuring the top of the high cross. I think they want to check sunrise today—it's equal-night day. So we haven't much time. They'll be moving down to the temple in about twelve minutes. Wolf needs to know."

Aaron whispered, "I'll go," and disappeared, slipping invisibly into the darkness. Even if they see him, they won't suspect him, Elwin thought. He produced a small cloth with ashes, and marked his own forehead with his thumb, then Stride's. "Any guards will be west of us, uphill. Your best three people there, the rest of us scattered with the prisoners, all right?'

"I should take two more and reinforce Wolf," Stride said. "Walker, you're in charge here."

They moved together to where the loyal prisoners were, foreheads marked, various weapons in their hands. Stride selected two young Eden men and moved out. Elwin moved about his men and women, saying, "You beside your suspected prisoners; you, two to each guard; you, come with me; may the Maker be with us."

Dawn was creeping from the east; faces could be recognized, gestures exchanged. As the group dispersed, other prisoners could be seen waking, turning heads.

***

At the cabin door, the construction boss, Strut, was standing with his two visitors from the Sun Tribe, Grim and Priest, and two armed guards. He had on his blue and yellow robe with the sun symbol on its chest. Priest had a robe just like it. Slubgob was there. So were Ruse and Diss.

"Hurry," said Priest. "It's a few minutes till sunrise. It <u>must</u> be perfectly aligned with the stone!"

Strut said, "I know, I know. We checked it yesterday; it was very close."

Priest said, "Close isn't good enough. It has to be perfect. People are going to be coming here, on this day for a thousand summers, to worship the Sun God."

Strut smiled, "The Sun God has been kind to us; it's going to be a clear morning. You know," he continued, sweeping his left arm outward, “After it’s finished, we’ll build a village here. Here we’ll have the guest house, for special visitors. And we’re going to clear and mark a road, all the way to your village on the seashore, for people who arrive there in boats to come here. We’re going to need a lot more slaves. We’ll be rich!”

“Hurry, now!” said Priest.

“All right, let’s go, Follow me.”

Behind them, Wolf cried, “Freedom! Freedom! Attack! Attack!” And a dozen others took up the cry.

Strut turned north towards the temple entrance, stopped in amazement at the sound, and had his head crushed by a massive club.

Now, seemingly, chaos ruled the camp. Strut’s three guards strode forward, their own clubs in their hands, to meet Wolf’s men. Eden’s young men rushed in, two to each guard, at the head, the legs, and the arms. The guards swung for heads with their clubs while the robed visitors shrank away, arms covering their heads.

It was an even fight for a few minutes. Deik swung at a guard, who side-stepped and struck him in the shoulder. As Deik fell, Aaron threw himself down against the guard’s knees. The guard fell. He was rising to his feet when Stride ran at him, fell on top of him, and turned him on his stomach. Two others caught him by the arms, but the guard was strong. They struggled until Arrow hit the guard’s head with a stone. Stride held him while he was tied up.

The other guards were soon overpowered. In the melee, three more of Stride’s attackers were hit - Abel, Thunder, and another bloody but standing. Suddenly, there were no more defenders. Strut was dead. Abel was unconscious. Grim and Priest were tied up, along with two guards. Ruse, Diss and Slubgob had disappeared in the confusion.

***

Down in the melee of prisoners, fighters, and guards, the battle lasted a little longer. The attackers had surprise and courage, but they were matched in number, as three of the prisoners joined the three guards, picking up stones to hit the attackers. Other prisoners milled around in terror or confusion, getting in the way. Walker's men pushed them aside but fought only with those who were fighting and had no blackened foreheads.

The prisoner fighters were soon struck down or just pushed away and surrounded. The guards fought with all their strength, in anger at these upstart prisoners, in deathly fear of their leaders.

But they were outfought. Wing was armed with fist-sized stones. He used two of them to throw down a guard, struck in the head and unconscious. The strongest guard was tripped by Walker and another. He tried to rise; Dog stood over him, slavering. Those down and alive were soon tied up with stout willow stems.

One guard had been sympathetic to his prisoners, withholding his worst blows, sometimes giving a little food to a hungry prisoner. He was identified early by Art, pushed over and sat on to keep him from choice and death.

The last club was dropped, and the last stone thrown. Quiet came upon the field. Sunlight streamed from the horizon across the giant stone cross-top, perfectly aligned, seen by no one. A bird sang. The battle was over.

At the tent, Elwin dropped his weapon, found Stride, and the two of them walked determinedly into the tent. Grim and Priest were held by Wolf's warriors, arms behind them, backs twisted into forced attention. Grim ducked his head and had it lifted up again by the hair. His face was twisted into a grin. Priest was pale with hands trembling.

Elwin's face shone like the sun. He said, "Will you now reject your murderous Sun God?"

Grim said nothing. Priest spoke, his voice a surprising whine coming from his imposing height and weight. "He will strike you dead."

Elwin looked at him with pity. He turned to include Grim. (Slubgob had fled.) "You swallowed Satan's sweet lies. You are his slaves. You gave yourselves into his keeping." And to Grim, "Your River Tribe toadys turned on my villagers, killed them, or made them slaves. What have you to say?"

Grim remained speechless. Priest sputtered, "My warriors will kill you all."

"Where is your village?"

"Don't touch me. We are many and—"

His speech was silenced by Stride's men, who took them both and hurried them away.

Elwin turned to Stride. "Keep them carefully. We will judge them when we are home again." Then he placed his hands on Stride's shoulders. "Stride, I'm so proud of you! We'll talk, after all is made straight, when it's time to make plans. I'll have an offer to make."

Stride swelled visibly at Elwin's words but bowed his head. "The Maker was with us. And your prisoners were incredible. How'd you get so many of them, all unknown to their leader?"

"We owe that to Abel and Gratia. Never have I heard such silver tongues or watched such seeing eyes."

"And the Devil's men have fled?

Elwin was grim. "Some of this bunch got away," he said, "but we'll track them down. And we'll deal with them."

"I'll be glad to help."

"We've got work to do now. Let's go down and see to the prisoners, get them organized. Come here to the tent this evening. We'll relax and talk."

That evening, in a cloud-brilliant spring sunset, Elwin's group settled outside the enemy's former headquarters to drink a little of their wine and talk.

"How is Abel?" asked Stride. "And Deik?"

"Abel's not good," said Elwin. "He was gashed by the guard he attacked. There was a lot of blood. Binta is with him now, inside. We'll go there when she comes for us. Deik will be well in time. But we lost three others, two killed in the assault here, and another prisoner, choked by a toady we didn't suspect. We have freed a hundred people, ours and others."

"And what of Satan himself?"

Elwin sighed. "I'd love to see him here, in chains. He was behind all this. The best we can hope for is to hold them at bay and wait for the Maker to return."

Gratia, who had disarmed a fighting prisoner and had her arm bandaged to show for it, said, "And meanwhile, for the Maker's angels to help keep us both good and safe. I know they are here. Maybe…" she was musing silently.

As if on cue, the dove fluttered down and stood before Gratia, looking from side to side at all of them, then back to her.

"Oh, Gaby!" she said. "We pray you give thanks to Him for standing with us."

Elwin spoke, "And, Gaby, will your master permit us to call him 'God'?"

Gaby nodded.

Elwin knelt down to the dove and asked, "Will you come to us as his messenger when we are fearful or confused, and bring us his counsel?"

The dove gave him a long look, nodded once, and flew off eastward into the morning sky.

Binta came to them, her own wounded leg bandaged. "Abel is weak but free from pain. And he wants to talk to you. I think just Elwin and Gratia."

They arose and went with her. Abel lay on a bed, head and shoulders propped, face white. He took Gratia's hand. She pressed it and said, "We are safe, dear Abel, thanks to you. Rest now."

Abel returned the pressure and spoke in a quiet whisper. "I do rest, and my rest may be long. But I have dreamed, and a vision of a greater battle came to me.

"In my dream, The Maker made space and time, and he called it the universe. Lucifer the Light-Bearer was his greatest angel, and the Maker promised him rule over space and time and all that was in it and gave him entry in and out of infinity/eternity where God rules with powers and multitudes we cannot even imagine. Lucifer was filled with pride, and thousands of angels were obedient to him.

"Then the Maker planned to fill His universe with living things, and to create humans to replenish and subdue and care for them. Unlike his angels, they would be born and die, for everything in space and time has a beginning and an end. But He would teach the humans to see and understand and love like Him and His angels.

"But here he made a choice. Humans must be born and die. But He would give us the power to make decisions and choices and ask only that we remain obedient to his teaching about what was good. And if we were faithful, He would bring us to life after death, to live with Him forever.

"Lucifer was enraged by this gift of God to humans.

"And so war came between the Maker and his finest creation. Lucifer told the Maker that He had made him supreme in space and time, and he would decide whether humans rose again or not. The Maker declared that this was rebellion, and he threw Lucifer and his angels out of always/everywhere into space/time and locked them there forever.

"But the Maker had given Lucifer great powers, and Lucifer, in his jealousy, set himself to destroy the humans. The Maker, with anguish, had to act to save them. I saw the Maker's anguish over what he would have to do."

Abel closed his eyes. "I will rest now."

They kissed him on his forehead and went away, and soon after, he died.

***

Night came, dark and cool. The freed slaves and their rescuers set a watch and settled down, most clustering together near the cabin. They sank into grateful sleep.

They were awakened by trembling in the ground beneath them. They rose, looked about in terror, and those near the temple ran into the open, away from its walls.

Inside the walls, the trembling was worse. The huge stones, so carefully arranged, danced on the rocking ground, fell, and cracked upon one another. The earth tremors diminished, and again, all was still. The sun rose upon the ruin of the temple.

50

Satan was in his cave. Diss and Ruse had been executed, their terror and despair an example to all his minions, and their bodies buried deep against discovery. His lieutenants sat with him: Beelzebub, Belial, and Mammon, in their bodies. Slubgob was gone, spared, but again, one of Belial's common soldiers.

He conquered his anger. Slowly, he looked from face to face with the authority of a judge. He said quietly, "A mistake was made. Beelzebub. What's the situation?"

"All our assets at the temple have died or fled," Beelzebub said. "Our caves in the east are intact, and our better men (yes, we have a few) are heading there. The status of our recruits in Adam's family and the River family is unknown; I have sent spies to scout and report. One or two of them may not have been betrayed."

"Mammon, the Universe?"

Mammon lifted his dark brows and stared into the distance. "All the stars are empty. As yet, there is no other life form to replace them." The eyes went down again.

Satan looked at each of them in turn and got no further responses. He crossed his knees, placed his hands atop them, and smiled, not a friendly smile.

"Well. We've had a little setback. Our preparations were going so well. Both villages were being infiltrated, and yes, the

River tribe was almost ready. But we attacked Adam's Village prematurely. It had not been adequately prepared. It had potential allies at the garden and was planning to find them. None of this was reported to me or taken into account. As a result, our effort at the temple has been wasted."

He paused then whirled toward them.

"We will not be defeated. When we have dealt with all the humans, I will ascend back into eternity and infinity. He will have to allow it. He will smile upon me again, and I shall resume my role as His eyes and His hands over all his realms. I'll do as I please! And I will bring you and the rest of my army up with me.

We will train our thousands of soldiers to make them tempters.

"Nothing else matters."

"But we can't just kill them," Beelzebub said. "The Maker has tied our hands."

"We have ways," Satan said. "We have them because of our victory in the garden. We have powers. They die; we don't. As it stands, they will not rise again. And they have made themselves bumblers—unable to escape their own greed, their lust, their envy of one another. We spread it, and it rises up within them—they know not how—an infection with no cure. We cannot kill them, but they can kill one another!

"They are confused about The Maker and can be made to distrust Him, even forget him. Then, even their virtues will be bent to the wrong ends. They will learn what this earth is made of, how its forces can be controlled. And they will say, 'See! It is our triumphs, not God, which can make us happy!' And those very triumphs we will twist to their destruction. They die. They die."

Beelzebub raised his head. "We'll teach them how to use government for the wealth of those who govern."

"We'll give them tools to experiment on themselves, bodies and minds," Mammon said. "They will use the results for wealth and pleasure, and they'll create new ways to kill and die."

And Belial stood up, arms outstretched. "Best of all! We'll keep fires burning under their distrust, jealousy, and hatred of one another. We'll teach them to make war on one another and to make the killings multiply!"

Satan, too, was on his feet. "I summarize. We cannot destroy them, but we can persuade them to destroy one another."

He moved, his hands up and down, up and out, his angels an audience becoming a mob.

"It will be a long plan. Meanwhile, their pain will be our food and drink. And this planet, so rich in beauty, will be their tomb, hot and dead and black."

He sat again. "Let's get to work."

51

Adam's people had returned to their village after the battle. Nineteen of them had died in the ambush by the River Tribe, in captivity, or in the final battle at the temple. In their place walked forty freed captives from other tribes who had elected to join Elwin's tribe instead of searching for the scattered remnants of their own.

Spring rains had covered much of the land between the forest and the stream with grasses and weeds, which Winnie was inspecting for herbs as many hands cleared and smoothed the land. Tents were being built anew and wooden houses shored up; teams were hunting for meat and gathering grains for bread and vegetables to boil and eat. Firewood was collected and dry-stored; the wine crew sought out containers. Art was busy making new tools.

The captives taken in battle were isolated in an improvised prison. A trial would occur after village repairs were tolerably complete.

Wing and two companions had headed east in haste from the temple on the long trek back to Eden.

Elwin and Gratia relaxed in the evening after a hard-working day back home. Maire joined them for a talk. Teller was still in Eden and Abel had died at the monument. They asked Walker to join them.

Gratia said, "I love relaxing here, in peace. I don't ever want there to be war again, here or anywhere. I wonder when Teller and the rest of them will come home."

Elwin smiled. "Yes, it's wonderful. But we have that trial to get through. Let's face it; nothing will ever be quite the same again." He turned to Walker. "It will be good to have you here to talk with us and tell us stories. You know the world better than we."

"It's good of you to invite me," Walker said, resting in his chair with Dog curled up on his feet. "I do have a lot of stories, and some of them may help you bring justice to those sinners. But as you feed on my adventures, I am feeding on your judgment. The trouble has made you wise."

"Thanks," said Elwin. "You know, different people have different ways of dealing with the world. Some of us try to figure out why things happen, others how they happen.

"Art takes things apart to see how they work. Teller puts them together to see what they mean."

There was a murmur of approval.

"So," said Maire, "What think you of our captives and their Sun God?"

Walker thought for a minute, then leaned forward. "Well, they're not the first humans to see a god behind every bush. It seems natural, when we don't have a notion why the sun and moon go round, what makes the wind blow or the winter follow the summer, to think that some unseen guide is behind each of these things."

"Yes," said Elwin, "and it's not necessarily in opposition to our one God, the Maker. He may have appointed assistants to move the wheels of earth and sky. I could believe it. If I had proof… if I could talk to these gods… if they could tell me how they do it."

Walker said, "There are a lot of gods believed in, but these are the first ones I've met who confound such a god with The God, the one who rules everything, the one who judges us. The results of that belief seem to be setting up one's own Great God, made in the image preferred by the power-hungry, set up to create wealth and power for some pretty ugly characters. There's a bad smell there."

"Yes," said Elwin. "I smell the creature who poisoned the fruit for Eve and Adam. Well… now we only have evils to hate, and thank God we hate them."

The trial was held, and the fomenters of sun-worship were condemned, but the judges could not find it in their hearts to spill more blood. Instead, they were stripped of their possessions and escorted far into the northern mountains by the hunters, there left to fend for themselves against the beasts, the winter, and their own moral confusions.

52

Wing and Ayo arrived in Eden to a joyful reunion with Tara and Teller and the other workers on the secrets of the stones, Eber and Karana. They got right to work.

Six days later, they went to Memo, and asked him and Teller to meet with them and hear what they had to say. Memo agreed and said that others interested could attend, too. They met in the conference space.

"Okay," said Eber, "Karana and I have studied the stones, and here's what we think.

"You remember about the forty-eight 'picts' in the first column and the sixteen 'shapes' in the second. We didn't know what they were. So we looked at the third column, the one in the new section of stone that you brought. It's different. Each row contains not just one but three, or four, or six, of the 'shapes' from column two. It seemed to us that these groups of shapes must be related to the Picts in column one. That these groups of shapes are an attempt to describe each Pict.

"Why describe each Pict?" said Wing. "You could capture what you say on a stone or a skin just using Picts. But boy, would you ever have to have a lot of Picts to describe everything!"

Then Karana had a great thought. She said, "When we look at a Pict, we say what it is—we make the sound of a word for that Pict. 'Man'—'baby'. Maybe the shapes stand for the sounds that a word makes. Maybe that's what writing IS. Then the second column items stand for sounds, and in the third column those sounds are strung together to sound like a word!"

"Tell them the rest, Karana!" She stepped forward, holding a sheepskin.

"Well, we spent a couple of days looking at shapes and making noises with our voices, and finally, we arrived at a sound that might go with each shape. And I got a sheepskin, nice and clean, and some old dark juice, and here's our list.

"There are three kinds of sounds we make. First, the long sounds:

A for 'ae' or 'ah.' E for 'ee' or 'eh.' I for 'eye' or 'ih.' O for 'oe' or 'uh.' U for 'ew' or 'oo.' Five shapes for six sounds. Then, the soft sounds:

J for 'juh' or 'zhuh.' L for 'luh.' M for 'muh.' N for 'nuh.' R for 'rruh.' S for 'ss' or 'zz.' W for 'wuh.' Seven shapes for nine sounds. Last, the hard sounds:

B for 'buh.' D for 'duh' or 'tuh.' F for 'fuh' or 'vuh.' G for 'guh' or 'kuh.'

Four shapes for seven sounds.

Teller asked, "Do you think sixteen sounds are enough?"

She thought for a moment. "Lots of people say words that sound a little different from others—especially strangers. And you noticed that some of our shapes cover pairs of similar sounds. You could make other shapes. But with these shapes and knowing what we want to say, I think we'll guess the right sounds."

Here are a few examples:

Pict of Man	M A N
Pict of Woman	W O M A N
Pict of Sun	S U N
Pict of rock	R O K (or maybe R A K)?

"We haven't started working out what the stone says—the main part of it. It just contains Shapes. LOTS of them! That might be a job for a Historian."

Memo laughed. "Let's start out together. You'll teach us as we go. Maybe we can make some progress before Teller and the others leave to return to their village."

And so they started. Each Pict was identified—"That's a deer!"; "That's a bowl!"—and the name given to each Pict was memorized by Wing and Eber.

Then each Shape was given its sound – A was spoken as 'ahh,' B as 'buh' (this was a hard adventure; they had no writing, they were inventing it.)

Then, the sounds in each row of the third column were "sounded out" together to make a "word" whose sound would match how the Pict in that row sounded when spoken. Of course, they knew how to say "deer" or "bowl." Now, they had a string of Shapes that would evoke that sound. D E R scratched into the stone would *mean* deer!

Now, to take on the stone's bulk, its spacious list of shapes/ sounds. Sometimes, the sounds marched close together, making it hard to group them into words. Sometimes, a word didn't have a Pict that matched the sound; it was a new word. Mistakes were made. Again, Wing and Eber had the job of memorizing the words as they flowed from the stone's sounds while Karana, care-filled, put them on her sheepskin. And so listened Memo and Teller, these experienced Historians, when they were invited to join the joyful group, unlocking the stories from human beginnings. The work wasn't done when Teller's group departed with cries of friendship. Memo promised to send messengers with a more finished product. But already the story of Eden was being filled with light and color and understanding.

53

"Memo," said Teller, grasping his hand and looking him in the eye, "Why don't you come with us? It's a long journey, but not a hurried one. And the seven of us will wait on you hand and foot."

Memo gave a great smile and returned the hand pressure.

"I'd love to see you all, but you can't carry me, and my body, alas, is not young enough to make that journey. Send some young ones here in a year or two to tell me how you do and whether you found the other stone."

"Memo, what will you do now that the excitement is over?"

Memo's face became serious. "Oh, as to that. I still believe strongly that the Maker allowed my ancestors to come back here for a reason. To remember, especially. To guard this place for what it stands for. To be here for travelers to return to and tell their stories. To pass on stories of adventures, and any hint of His return. That will keep us busy and—useful, don't you think?"

"I do," said Teller, "and I promise that you'll hear from us again. It will give me pleasure just to know you're here, my courteous, welcoming friend. Goodbye. May the years treat you lightly."

"Begone!" said Memo, with a tear in his voice.

***

Teller and his companions were home at last in the cool of autumn, dusty and tired from their long trek west, and they rejoined their old friends as well as the new villagers. They were welcomed with hugs of joy, and a large group gathered on the next Rest Day to hear their story. Memo had allowed two boys and a girl to come along with Teller, Ayo, Wing, and Tara, making a new Group of Seven, not counting Tara's baby.

Teller told of the happenings at Eden since the war party had left and gave everyone a beautiful description of the garden. He recounted the efforts of Wing, Eber, and Karana to unlock the message in the stones. The first part of the story had been deciphered.

"It was hard going, with some guesses and some mistakes, but oh, my! Listen to our Father and Mother speaking to us!"

The Maker said to Adam and Eve:

"You are the first of my creatures on Earth to whom I have given the gifts of self-awareness, language, reasoning, and the knowledge to do what is right. You have much to learn, and while we are together in the garden, I will begin to teach you. I will not withhold knowledge deliberately to keep you subject to me. But I cannot teach you everything because your minds would not understand them.

"I will give you your first tools. You will use them to study this world and the creatures in it. Then, with new tools you will discover, your children's children will unlock its secrets."

"What tools will you give us?" the Father asked.

"Words first," The Maker said. "I have awakened you with words already in your heads. Words are your first tools. Names for all the things you will see on earth and in the skies and for the living things. Doing words to describe what happens. Measuring words to describe things by their size and weight. Words to say how things look and feel and smell and taste, and very important words to say how you feel—love, fear, joy, all the colors and tastes of life.

"Since you have language, you already know some of these things.

"From language, you must build a world of knowledge so that your sons and daughters can start with what you have seen and found and move further. Your knowledge must be preserved—first in memory, in stories that will be told for thousands of years. Later, you will discover how to freeze knowledge in things so that other people can look at them and hear your words."

"What does 'freeze' mean?" asked Eve.

The Maker laughed. "Oh, there is so much to learn. When the earth grows so cold that the water in ponds and lakes becomes solid and painful to touch, what do you call it?"

"My mind tells me that it is 'ice.'

"When the cold *freezes* water, it is ice. If it freezes you, you die."

"What is it to 'die'?"

"That is enough learning for today," The Maker said.

All seemed well. Then somehow, when the Parents were proud and strong in their new knowledge and the Maker had left them for a while, Satan came.

In the garden, the two were resting and talking about what they had learned when there appeared a man. He was tall and handsome, with a black beard neatly cut and smiling dark eyes.

"Hello, I am Lucifer," he said.

"Oh!" said Adam. "You surprised us. I thought we were the only ones of us, so far."

Lucifer chuckled. "I believe you are, except for me. I've been around for quite a while. The Maker used me for practice before making you."

Eve looked at him curiously. "Well, you look very nice." She glanced at Adam. "We were just talking about that tree and why we mustn't touch its fruit."

"Oh, that," Lucifer said. "It's marvelous fruit, you know. Eating it opens your eyes to things. Makes you *know* a lot of things. It did that to me."

"You ate some?" said Adam. "Didn't the Maker forbid it? He said it was dangerous."

"Yes, he did. That's a test, you see."

"A test?"

"Yes, a trial to show that you can work things out for yourselves."

Eve frowned. "Shouldn't we wait for Him to tell us that?"

"Oh, no. He wants you to show Him that you've grown up and are ready to decide things for yourself. He was so proud of me when I did it."

The man smiled warmly at both of them.

"I think we should wait," Eve said.

"I'm not sure," said Adam.

"Well…

Go ahead, try some." He reached out to the tree, picked some fruit, and handed it to Eve. "Here you go."

"Well, if you say so." She handed one to Adam, and they both bit in. She swallowed and paused, then looked around, confused and scared.

"Oh, yes …. Dear Adam, what have I done?"

Adam clutched her arm in fear, and as he looked about, he saw the handsome man shrink and slither away.

When the Maker returned to them, he wept. He told the Parents that they and all their children had been poisoned by eating the fruit unprepared—which had poured horrors into their minds, overpowered them with hard, horrible truths and lies of greed, anger, lust—before they were strong enough to know what they meant and how to handle them. They knew now that they were going to die and that life after death was blocked for them. Worst of all, this weakness meant that he, the Maker, could no longer keep them here, lest they eat of the Tree of Life.

They must leave the garden and make their way without the Maker by their side.

"Worst of all, you have lost the ability to live again after death.

"We separate now," He said. You must go out into Earth, unprepared, and scratch a living from it. And I may not speak to you directly, as I am doing now. Many of your descendants will forget me, and strange fragments of your story will be believed. Men will tell stories of many Makers—but all of them will be me. Except that the terrible ones will be the Devil, Satan, whom you believed. Now, your job is to remember this story, tell it to your children, and never forget who I am."

"Then all is lost," said Eve.

"No," The Maker said. "All is endangered, and but for Me all would be lost. And I fear a long exile it is to be. But I will come for you in time. I will open life after death to you again."

"Why must it be so long?" Adam asked. "Is it punishment?"

"It is your punishment," The Maker replied, "but not simply that. There is a great battle raging in my realm. I have made laws and promises, not only here in time and space but in always and everywhere, where I rule over many spirits. All these promises must be kept. In this battle, I cannot now destroy the evil without also destroying the good. To change that will require a terrible sacrifice. You must be patient. I will come.

"I know you are confused by this. Your minds are marvelous, but they are not the minds of angels, and cannot completely encompass infinity and eternity. You must use comparisons to think about these truths. 'God is like... or Heaven is like...'

"But you do not have to completely understand in order to believe. Believe that I love you and will return to save you from the effects of your sin.

"And this will be the end: My Son will become one of you, and die and live again that uou may do the same.

"And in the end, Lucifer will lay his sword upon the ground before my throne.

"For you, remember just this: Love me, obey me, love one another."

Teller said, "That is what we learned from the stone. So, the sin of Satan corrupted space and time, and the sin of our Parents corrupted us. Our Maker has promised to return. Our enemy Satan is still in this universe, condemned to remain here, but he will be defeated. How? I don't know. I cannot see the future."

Elwin said, "In a way, the story on the stone has shattered me."

"It seems that way at first," Teller said. "But it confirms what we suspected and explains our sorrows."

"It does. And it gives us hope."

54

Stride came to Elwin's house the next morning, asking for a brief conversation. Gratia welcomed him in and retrieved Elwin from behind the house, where he was plastering a wall.

"It's good to have you back!" Elwin said, clasping Stride's hand. "Thanks for leading the prisoners out of exile."

"It's good to be back, sir. It's good to have so much trouble behind us. When I think how naïve I was, I … just don't know what to say!"

Elwin chuckled. "We've all become wiser. And I still can't forecast what's ahead. There's a saying from a man hundreds of years ago:

'At evening, are we wise
Of this day's joy and sorrow?
Not wise enough to see
Just what will come tomorrow!'

"We just have to thank our God-in-Chief for today and carry on. Do you remember me saying, after the battle, that I had something in store for you?"

"I do, sir. And I have a plan to tell you about today. One I would like your permission to carry out."

"Ah, we have surprises for each other. Gifts to exchange, perhaps. What I wanted to ask you was whether you would consider becoming my second-in-command here, and my heir, to become Village Leader when I die."

Stride's mouth opened in total surprise. "Sir, I don't think—I'm not ready for such… for that."

Elwin smiled. "Maybe not quite, but you will be. You have courage, strength, and honesty—and now wisdom. Now tell me what's in your mind."

Stride said, "I feel a little dizzy. But I will tell you. A group of us want to do a Parting."

"Oh, my. Tell me who, when, and why—what your vision is."

"We learned so much on our trek east to Eden. We realized how little of this world we know. We still have the urge to learn more. Myself and Binta. And Winnie and Art want to come, and so does Walker, and so do Kelso and Karana! Oh, and young Aaron wants to come too, and we think he's earned the chance with his courage in the battle. We heard, at Eden, that there's a sea-faring village at the top of the Inmost Sea, and they might have a stone, and we want to visit them and join them for a while maybe. And I want to marry Binta, and she wants to marry me."

Elwin and Gratia just stared at one another, mouths open. Then they laughed together.

"That's amazing, young man. What I'm thinking is this. Go on your new adventure; you know how to lead and what to expect. And if after that adventure you want to return to us and take up my offer, that would fit perfectly. And if you don't, you'll do something else even better. Will I marry you two before you go?"

"Oh yes, sir. Thank you!" Stride looked thoughtful. "Tara wished she could come too. But of course, she has the baby."

Gratia leaned forward, hands clasped. "Oh, I wish Tara had Priam still!"

Elwin said, "Yes, she's been so strong and faithful. And we don't know what happened to Priam. After the battle, he just disappeared again. Perhaps another young man will see her and love her."

That evening, Elwin said to Walker, "I'll miss you in our group of listeners. I guess you still have that urge to travel."

Walker said, "Elwin, I love it here with you, but I decided on one more trip for the help I can be to these travelers. I will return, and if they have a stone up there at the top of the sea, I'll bring it back to you. You've not seen the last of me."

"Ah, that's a generous thing to do. Just know that your place at this table will be kept."

On the next Rest Day were celebrated the weddings and the Parting.

Binta and Stride stood before Elwin, hands joined. Next to them, Winnie and Artisan did the same.

Elwin said, "In all our struggles, we have learned that family is our right center. Family makes children and teaches them how to live. Family holds the love of our God, the Maker. Families together decide on our laws and customs. They help one another, no matter what. Remember this:

"The family is greater than the law and older than the tribe."

He looked at them, one at a time.

"Do you promise to love each other?" Together both pairs said, "We do."

"Will you live in accordance with our customs?"

"We will."

To the audience, the parents, friends, everyone who knew Winnie and Artisan and Stride and the fewer who knew Binta: "Does anyone have reason against this marriage?" No one spoke.

"Then I pronounce each of you married and a family under God." He placed his hands on their shoulders, one pair at a time, and there was cheering and laughter.

Food and wine had been provided, and conversations flourished. Soon the young people of the village raised their voices in a dancing song led by Ayo:

Do-re-mi-do-re-me bubble and say
Beedle and tweedle and wheedle away

Tickety-tockety tap on a Tree
Tangle your toes up and slap on your knee
Slap 'em and clap 'em and happy we'll be!

Show me sweet sister how high can you jump?
Tap it and twirl it and give it a thump
Tickle me tackle me turn me around
Take me and shake me and down to the ground!

And later, another song;
Boys up and clap! (boys clap)
Girls give a Wow! (wow)
Boys once again!
Girls do it now!
Clap! Clap! Yay! Yay!
Wow! Wow! Yay! Yay!
Never a doubt! Dance all about!
Roll around roll around
Stop with a shout!

After enough time for the new couples to be thoroughly congratulated, Elwin called again for silence, and the new Seven plus one were called to the front. There they stood in line abreast: Binta, Stride, Winnie, Artisan, Walker, Karana from the Eden Tribe who could read the stone, young Kelso who had escaped from Mithra-Ko and helped prepare the rescuers for the battle, and even younger Aaron, who wanted to learn more of this marvelous world.

Walker's Dog was beside him with his new mate, Lady, who had just walked in from the forest to the village and right up to Dog as if she owned him.

Now Elwin signaled Teller, who stood before the travelers.

He said, "A year ago, seven of us made a journey from here to Eden, with a life's worth of adventure and danger, to a good conclusion. Now, with new companions, you will set out westward on a new adventure. The people at the north end of the Inmost Sea, as far as we know, are those who departed from our ancestors long ago, and have communicated once with Hunter and Memo of Eden. We think they may have another stone, and two of you have studied with Wing and his friends on how to interpret it. It may not exist or be the same as the first two, but whether or not, we hope you will bring it back to us. And indeed, all or any of you will be welcomed back if you decide to leave their village or if they reject you.

"The world seems boundless, and most of it is still unknown to us. May you remember us and our story. Kelso has agreed to be your Historian and keep your adventures in his mind and perhaps on clay or a stone. May the Maker go with you, and may we meet again!"

And with much ceremony and many expressions of love, the new Seven plus one departed.

***

That night, a man dressed in the rags of an old cloak, barefoot, crept up to the stream at the north, downstream edge of the village and stood, gazing at the ground. His body was skin and bones, bent with fatigue; his face, if you could see it in the darkness, was grim with purpose. He washed himself, found a nearby hollow, and slept.

Priam awoke with the sun. He rose and moved quietly to a spot in the trees where he could see Elwin's house. When Elwin came out, yawning, and sat by the table, Priam approached him, circling to the front, not to surprise him. He stood silent.

Elwin peered, and recognition came into his eyes. "Priam," he said, "You've come back to us at last. We thought you were dead. Please sit down."

Gratia had come out, and she sat next to Elwin.

"Tell us your story," said Elwin gently.

Priam sat upright, hands on thighs. "I'm not dead. Sometimes, I wished I was. But I escaped, hid alone, and thought about my life. How I threw away what was best. I've come back to find Tara, throw myself down before her, and tell her my fault and failure."

Gratia said, "Tara is here."

Elwin said, "Have a little food, wear a cloak I will bring you, then if you wish, we'll bring her here."

Priam silently nodded in fealty and obedience.

Tara came, took him in her arms, and placed in his arms their daughter, Lucy.

***

Later, Gratia and Elwin sat together.

"This last year's been such a whirlwind!" Gratia sighed. "And these last days have been a wonderful ending. Now I'm happy just to rest. And we'll miss those travelers. But this trip won't be an escape, just an adventure."

Elwin said, "I made a poem for you for your birthday. Want to hear it?"

"That would be lovely."

He closed his eyes for several seconds, then cleared his throat.

"If heaven is milk and honey,
And everything is free,
Will the great banquet have no taste,
Taken so easily?

How will our Maker, God, combine
The victory with the chase?
How could it fill us not to run
But still to win the race?

How would our love be strong and stout,
A tree above the plain,
If growing it had been without
The stimulus of pain?

The drops that water us are tears,
The sun is goals beyond our range;
And we are ploughed by discontent
And fertilized by change.

Our very bones, unless they break,
Are stronger for the stress;
For every blow we've dealt or met
I love you more, not less.

God will but smile and answer, 'See
That sequence, rhythm, rhyme,
Anticipation, memory
Are artifacts of time.

Here in the center, all is now—
Sit down with me and sup;
The battle and the victory
Are blended in the cup."

She took his hand and tearfully smiled her thanks.

55

Enoch stood braced against the wind, the rain in his face, gazing northward across the coast to the North Sea, where that wind was whipping the water into waves and spray. He was glad that his boat had not ventured out upon the waters today. They'd fished from the shore; their catch lay upon the beach.

"Methuselah!" he cried to his young son, who was at the shoreline testing the waves with his feet. "Come now! It's time to walk home."

Enoch's family was a long way from the land that had been home in their great-grandparents' time. Three hundred years ago, they had left the Great River in search of peace. According to the story, another family, large, prosperous, and aggressive, had come up the Great River from far to the south, calling themselves the Great Family and claiming the allegiance of any others they encountered. Enoch's family had attempted to live with them. But their tools disappeared, their daughters were collected as brides, and their memories of the Maker scorned. Rather than worship the Sun God and obey his priests, they had hurried westward under cover of night to the Inmost Sea, where, for a season, there was peace.

But the arm of the Great Family was long. Soon Enoch's family found themselves harassed again, pushed ever farther north along the eastern shore. But they stayed together and stayed to themselves. They did encounter two other families but kept their distance and continued northward year after year. They became skilled fishermen, wading deep with spears and nets into the pleasant salt water (warmer now, for the summers had begun to grow warmer.) One year, one of the boys had learned to mount a log, break off its branches, paddle up the estuary of a river, and out into the sea a hundred feet or so before he fell off and had to swim to shore, laughed at by his brothers. But the idea fascinated them all. By the time their sons were strong, a way to lash sticks together had been devised, and paddles, and in another generation, the family was pulling its boat northward and westward with them on their summer treks. They saw how birds rode the wind out westward across the endless water but did not know how to use that wind-power.

Still, this family became real seafarers by the time they had migrated westward along the north shore to where the Inmost Sea sloped north-westward, soon revealing islands not far out. Then, the shore swung to the northeast up a narrow channel toward a smaller (but still great) body of water. They were finally blocked from it by a broad bridge of land stretching from east to west and a mile thick, with the Great North Sea on the north side of it. The land bridge was beautiful and safe and empty of other human life, and here they stayed. They camped near the south end of what they called the Bridge, along the banks of a finger of water which ran from the Inmost Sea north into the Bridge, almost cutting it in two. They called it the Bay, and kept their boat there, and began to build another.

They called themselves now "The Seafarers."

***

Enoch and Methuselah took two hours to walk leisurely home with their catch, where a fresh meal was prepared and enjoyed. Then Enoch gathered the family for a story.

"One reason we left the Great River," said Enoch, "was the greed of the Great Family for treasures. We found we had to hide anything of beauty or usefulness, or they would simply take it. We had a few very old family things we wanted badly to keep. For instance, this stone." He pulled from his pouch a flat glass-black stone with strange markings on both sides. "We've had this since we left our old family to move to the river ten lifetimes ago."

The family had heard this story before, but they were always interested.

"What are the markings for?" asked Methuselah, the youngest but most curious son.

"We don't know," Enoch replied. "It's not in any of the stories. But the stories say that we came away from a place far east of here, in the mountains beyond the North Sea. So, when my grandfather Enos was our leader, he sent two young men eastward to try to find that place. They were gone from early summer until the next summer was almost gone, and returned full of stories. They had found a family in the mountains which had a stone like ours. They couldn't read theirs either, and Enoch hadn't given ours to the boys, fearing they'd lose it. So they just told our story, and the family in the mountain promised that some day they'd come to the Inmost Sea and find us."

"But they never have," muttered another man, an old one. "I remember those boys. They were good boys, older than me and wild. They always wanted to go exploring again. They said they 'had the wanderlust.' And one spring, they left again, to go west. That's the last we saw of them."

There was a thoughtful silence after that. Some of the boys were obviously wondering whether they wanted to go west and explore.

***

The next morning, in the distance, they saw and heard humans coming towards them along the strip of land between the seas. Peering into the sunlight, they could make out eight people, men and women, apparently unarmed. Enoch raised his arms, hands empty, in welcome as they neared.

Stride was the first to reach him. “Thanks for your welcome,” he said. “We had word that you were here and have traveled far to meet you. We come in peace.”

“Come, I’ll show you around. I want you to go see the new boat we’re building. But first, how about some food and drink?” And off they went to meet Enoch’s family.